CONTENTS

INTRODUCTION

I strongly believe that everyone's journey with diabetes is different. However, even with all the complications of diabetes, nothing should stop you from enjoying life or doing the things that you love. That's the way it should be!

I have mentioned several times in my cookbooks that, as a registered dietitian, I hate seeing people get enslaved by their dietary habits. Diabetes is a chronic condition that, over the last couple of years, has become widespread. One thing that is driving the proliferation of diabetes cases is our lifestyle and the changing dietary habits.

We've become so busy in our work life that we don't have time to prepare nice, healthy meals at home. As a result, we depend largely on fast foods, and this is where the rain started beating us.

Because of our poor dietary habits, we are at crossroads with our health, and conditions like diabetes are now a permanent fixture.

But that's not what worries me most. What worries me is the community that has gone all out to make healthy eating difficult for people of all walks. Besides, I'm always gutted when I dive online, only to find a sea of dieting information and plenty of fads that misled and trap many in poor eating habits.

I sat down and thought, how can we save people from the jaws of the confusing web of food? The option was to create a cookbook with easy to cook, delicious, and completely versatile meals. This cookbook will give you all the information you need to know about diabetes from Type 1 and Type 2 diabetes to gestational diabetes. Most importantly, I will introduce you to one of the fascinating cooking appliances: the crockpot.

Additionally, you will find easy recipes to keep on the path to a healthier, fun, and long life with diabetes. The plan will help you eat healthier without breaking the bank. I choose 5 ingredients or less meals to make cooking easy for everyone.

Whether you have diabetes or have a friend or family with diabetes, this cookbook has the information you need to make life with diabetes sustainable. I am pretty sure that you won't get bored, and you'll scale above the hurdles of diabetes to enjoy your life. This is the key to a happy and satisfying life with diabetes.

Diabetes 101

According to the American Diabetes Association, <u>30.3 million Us citizens or 9.4%</u> of the population had diabetes in 2015. Needless to say, this number is getting even bigger as the days go by. This is a worrying stat, but its reality we all are grappling with.

Now, if you aren't amongst the 30.3 million people with diabetes, you probably have a close relative or friend with it. This means if we are to deal with this rampaging menace, we have to join hands and deliver the telling impact of our collective efforts.

However, keeping diabetes under control is not a cakewalk, especially when you consider the modern eating habits. But we can't let our own eating habits drive us into the grave. As a result, we have to keep fighting until the diabetes menace shows us its back. But, as you know, to solve any problem you must get to the bottom of it and understand its root cause.

It's because of this reason that I have written this introductory chapter to introduce you to diabetes.

Let's roll!

What is Diabetes?

Diabetes mellitus or simply diabetes is a widespread health condition where the blood sugar is too high. Actually, diabetes is a cluster of health conditions that inhibits the production of insulin or cause insulin not to work properly or a combination of the two. When either or both of these insulin complications strike, they cause the blood sugar to accumulate to harmful levels, hence diabetes.

To understand diabetes better, you first have to understand how insulin is produced and used in the body. Insulin is produced in the pancreas by cells known as the islet of Langerhans, which are spread throughout the pancreas. 75% of these cells make insulin whereas, 20% produce glucagon.

Insulin is tasked with maintaining the blood glucose within the healthy levels. On the other hand, glucagon raises blood sugar level. From this, you can see the function of the pancreas cell is counterproductive when it comes to controlling diabetes.

What happens is, when food is metabolized normally, the pancreas releases insulin to counteract the rising blood glucose levels. When insulin levels fall, less glucose is stored in the form of glycogen, hence the build-up.

The cases of diabetes have proliferated in recent times, impelled by unhealthy eating habits. This doesn't mean the diabetes is entirely new; actually, the chronic condition has been around since 100 AD. The term diabetes was coined from the Greek word for "flow-through." Primarily, the condition was described by its two core symptoms urinating frequently and extreme thirst.

Turning Diabetes Around

There are three types of diabetes you need to know. They include:

Type 1 Diabetes

Initially, the type one diabetes was known as insulin-dependent diabetes mellitus (IDDM). It's a condition where the pancreas makes hardly any insulin or no insulin at all. Unfortunately, the causes of type 1 diabetes remain unknown.

Health experts believe that type 1 diabetes is an autoimmune disease. This means that a condition causes the immune system to suppress the normal functioning or destroy the islet of Langerhans. As a result, the body is unable to produce enough insulin to regulate blood sugar.

Type 1 diabetes is widespread in young adults and children. This is the reason it was known by the term juvenile-onset diabetes. Generally, people with this type 1 diabetes have to inject insulin into their bodies to keep the condition under control.

Symptoms Of Type 1 Diabetes

- Frequent urination
- Increased thirst
- Fatigues and weakness
- Extreme hunger

- Mood changes such as irritability
- Unintended weight loss
- Blurred vision.

Foods For Type 1 Diabetes

Initially, health experts thought there was a special group of food for people with diabetes. They believed that people who have diabetes had to avoid certain foods like foods with sugar. However, that seemed not to be the case, especially for people with type 1 diabetes.

Indeed, people with type 1 diabetes can eat the same foods as everyone, provided that the meals are healthy. The only difference is that they have to cut the consumption of unhealthy fat and eat foods with plenty of fiber.

Type 2 Diabetes

Type 2 diabetes was commonly known as non-insulin-dependent diabetes mellitus (NIDDM). With type 2 diabetes, the pancreas produces insulin, but the amount is not enough to regulate blood sugar. In other cases, the pancreas produces insulin in large quantities, but the body, for some reason, cannot utilize it properly.

Unlike type 1 diabetes, type 2 diabetes is widespread in adults over 40 years old, hence the name of adult-onset diabetes. In most cases, type 2 diabetes is common in overweight people or those from a family with a history of diabetes.

Interestingly, 90% of diabetes cases are type 2 diabetes. Besides, 80% of type 2 diabetes patients are overweight. This is the reason why being overweight is seen as a trigger of type 2 diabetes. People with type 2 diabetes can control this condition with weight control. This means adopting proper dieting and a strict exercise regimen to achieve weight control.

Also, in most cases, people with type 2 diabetes do not need to inject insulin to manage their conditions. In some serious case, it takes the combination of weight control, oral medication, and insulin injection to control type 2 diabetes.

Symptoms Of Type 2 Diabetes

All type 1 diabetes symptoms are type 2 diabetes symptoms. Other symptoms include:

- Slow healing of wounds and cuts
- Numbness, tingling, or pain in feet and hands.
- Yeast infection and itching
- Patches of dark skin

Foods For Type 2 Diabetes

People with type 2 diabetes can take meals with varying ratios of protein, fats, and carbohydrates. The proteins and fats should primarily be obtained from plant sources. On the other hand, carbohydrates should come from low glycemic foods like vegetables.

Gestational

The third type of diabetes is known as gestational diabetes, which occurs during pregnancy. What happens is that during pregnancy, there are a lot of hormonal changes. Some of these changes may cause a build-up of blood glucose. In other cases, the demand for insulin rises, and the pancreas is unable to keep up with the demand.

One interesting fact is that nearly a third of women with gestational diabetes are highly likely to develop type 2 diabetes. Also, since it occurs during pregnancy, it's difficult to deal with it using oral medication. This is because oral drugs can affect the fetus. The best way to deal with gestational diabetes is proper dieting and exercise. In some serious cases, insulin injection is required to lower blood glucose.

The symptoms of gestational diabetes include unusual thirst, fatigue, frequent urination, and sugar in the urine. Luckily, these symptoms fade away when the baby is born.

Packing Power Into Every Meal

What you need to know is that diabetes has no cure. However, with the right care and attention, you can keep it under control. This means making unique lifestyle commitments, constantly monitoring blood sugar, and adopting proper exercise routine. Above all, you must curb the poor dietary habits and pack power into every meal you take.

As you may have noticed, medical nutrition therapy is of paramount importance when it comes to diabetes management. Unfortunately, there are a lot of misconceptions concerning diabetes and nutrition. In this chapter, we'll reveal the details you need to know about diabetes and the core nutrients.

Carbohydrates

Studies have shown that people with diabetes need to consume foods containing normal carbohydrates. In particular, people with diabetes should endeavor to eat carbs from fruits, whole grain, low-fat milk, and vegetables.

So, how many carbs should people with diabetes eat?

One thing you need to know is that there is no "one size fits all" carbs level for everyone. Why? Because our bodies are created to be different. Besides, there are other significant factors to put into consideration when deciding the carb count, including weight, gender, activity level, and age.

What we know is that people with diabetes should obtain 45% of their calories from carbohydrates. For example, women with diabetes need 3 - 4 servings per meal. On the other hand, men require 4-5 carbs servings per meal. One carb serving is equal to 15g per serving.

To be on the safe side, work with qualified medical professionals, and dietitians to establish the exact carb goal. You also need to constantly count carbs to maintain your blood sugar levels within a healthy range.

Proteins

Proteins help your body grow and are as vital as other macronutrients. Because of this, people with diabetes need to consume proteins. However, they need to understand what happens when you consume proteins.

As mentioned earlier, protein helps the body develop new tissues. But besides this, protein is broken into glucose, which is used for energy in the body. However, unlike carbohydrates, proteins are metabolized into glucose less efficiently. Consequently, the impact of protein on the level of glucose in the blood may take a few to several hours to occur.

People with diabetes need to take into account the effects of protein before taking protein-based meals. It's advisable that you understand how the sugar levels may react to such meals. This will help you know the exact insulin requirements for your body.

The recommended protein intake varies by age:

- 1-3 years: 15 grams
- 4-6 years: 20 grams
- 7 -10 years: 28 grams
- 11-14 years: 42 grams
- 15-18 years: 55 grams
- 19-50 years: 55 grams
- Over 50 years: 53 grams

Dietary Fat

Fat, like carbohydrates, get a lot of attention when it comes to diabetes management. There is no doubt diabetics need to control their fat intake to curb the risk of developing heart disease. More crucial than the total fat is the type (healthy or unhealthy) of fat you consume. Not all fats are good for you, that's why it's important to learn the difference.

Unhealthy Fats

Unhealthy fats include saturated fats from foods like high-fat dairy products, high-fat meats, lard, butter, chocolate, cream sauces, and poultry skin. The goal should be to consume less than 10% of calories from these types of foods.

Other unhealthy fats include trans-fat and cholesterol. One thing to know about trans-fat is that they increase cholesterol levels in the blood. This type of fat is worse than saturated fat, and you should eat as less trans fats as you can. Trans fat is contained in processed foods, stick margarine, and fast foods. On the other hand, cholesterol is contained in high-fat meat, poultry skin, egg yolk, and high-fat dairy products.

Healthy Fats

Whether you have diabetes or not, you should eat the following healthy fats. One is monounsaturated fat, which is also known as healthy or good fats. This type of fat lowers bad (LDL) cholesterol. Foods that contain monounsaturated fats include canola oil, avocado, olive oil, nuts, peanut butter & oil, and sesame seeds.

Another type of healthy fat is polyunsaturated fat, which is obtained from plant-based oil, walnuts, salad dressings, sunflower oil, mayonnaise, and soft margarine. Besides, you should eat omega3 fatty acids from foods like herring, mackerel, albacore tuna, salmon, rainbow trout, and sardines.

Complete Nutrition For Diabetics

Now that you know the nutrients you need to manage diabetes, it's time to look into the healthy food groups for diabetes. Remember, the foods you consume makes a big difference in the way you manage diabetes. Besides, the foods contribute greatly to how well you feel and how much energy you gain.

There are four main food groups for people with diabetes. They include:

Vegetable and Fruits

Naturally, veggies and fruits pack a punch in terms of fiber, minerals, and vitamins. Not just that, fruits and veggies contain low calories, which is good for people with diabetes. In fact, living with diabetes should not stop you from eating fruits and vegetables.

You have them the way you want, dried, fresh, canned, or frozen. You should try to eat a variety of fruits to get as many minerals and vitamins as possible. However, try to avoid smoothies and juices; they offer no value in terms of fiber content.

One thing to note is that, as much as you try to limit the number of carbs you consume, you need to include fruits and veggies in your meals. Having them in your meal protects against heart disease, some types of cancers, stroke, and high blood pressure.

Starchy Foods

Starch is obtained from rice, potatoes, pasta, naan, chapattis, and plantain. These foods provided glucose, which is broken down in the body for energy. While glucose is needed to power the body cells, getting it in high quantities can be detrimental to the health of people with diabetes.

Some starchy foods can cause a sudden rise in blood glucose levels. These foods are known as high glycemic index foods and should be avoided by people with diabetes. This doesn't mean you should not consumer starchy foods. There are better foods with a low glycemic level like whole grains, wild rice, and brown rice.

Proteins

We discussed proteins in our previous topic. One thing we can add is that diabetics, like other people, need to eat the correct amount of proteins. Besides, helping your muscles grow, proteins protect your heart health. As such, you should eat proteins every day. Primarily, aim at eating at most 2 portions of oily fish each week.

Oils And Spreads

As mentioned earlier, you need to eat less saturated fat. This way, you will lower cholesterol, hence curb the risk of stroke and heart disease.

Crockpot 101

What is Crockpot?

In our cookbook, we'll reveal some of the most delicious meals you can cook using your crockpot. This is one of the most used kitchen appliances, and it comes in handy in the fall and winter.

So, do you really know what a crockpot is?

To better understand what a crockpot is, you must first understand what a slow cooker is. As the name suggests, a slow cooker is a kitchen appliance that cooks food slowly. In other words, a slow cooker uses moist heat to cook food, usually, over a long time. For example, cooking stew on a stove takes at most two hours, but with a slow cooker this can take up to 10 hours.

Now back to the crux of this topic, what is a crockpot. You will be surprised to know that a crockpot and a slow cooker perform the same function. They are multicookers that use electricity and moist heat for cooking food. As a result, they make foods super tender and integrate the flavors more strongly than in short-term cooking.

The name crockpot is a term trademarked by Rival Manufacturing Company when they introduced the cooker in 1971. Since this term is a registered trademark, the rival manufacturer opted to use the word "slow cooker" to avoid legal disputes. This gave birth to the slow cooker we see today.

Interestingly, all crockpots are slow cookers, but not all slow cookers are crockpots. So, what's the difference between a crockpot and a slow cooker? This is not the easiest topic in the world of kitchen appliances. In fact, it almost difficult to differentiate between the two. The reason is simple: both terms are used interchangeably. One difference is probably the design. The crockpot has a ceramic or porcelain pot inside, whereas the slow cooker has a metal pot. Besides, the crockpot has heating elements at the bottom and on the sides, which is not the case with slow cookers.

The Features And Functions of a Crock pot

A crockpot, like the slow cooker, has three main parts: the pot, the lid, and the heating elements.

Pot

In most cases, crockpots come with an oval ceramic pot. This shape makes it easy for the pot to accommodate large chunks of roasts and meat.

The Lid

The crockpot lid can be made of glass or clear plastic. The reason it's clear is to help you monitor the progress of the meal you are cooking without having to open the pot.

Other notable, crockpot functions include:

Heat Settings

Generally, crockpots have only two temperature settings. There is a LOW option that brings foods to temperatures, not above 200 degrees Fahrenheit. On the other hand, there is a HIGH option that brings food to a temperature of up to 300 degrees Fahrenheit. Some crockpot brands have a third temperature setting, a low-wattage, warming option.

Timer

Thanks to the advancement made in crockpots, it's possible to find brands with a timer. The time helps you to cook food for a specified period.

Tips For a Better Experience With a Crockpot

Since you will be using your crockpot to make all our recipes, its good you learn the tricks and tips to have an excellent experience with the appliance. Here are some tips to give you the best crockpot experience:

1.   Always start by preheating your crockpot.
2.   When cooking meat, start with room temperatures
3.   For amazing flavors, add caramelized bits to the bottom of your crockpot.
4.   For amazing texture, add gingerbread cookies when cooking meat dishes
5.   Fill the pot two-thirds to three-quarters full.
6.   Always trim fat from meat before cooking them in a crockpot.

BREAKFAST & BRUNCH

1.   Apple & Pumpkin Oatmeal

Servings: 4
Cooking Time: 6 Hours
Ingredients:
- 1 ½ cups water
- ½ cup apple juice, sugar-free
- ½ cup pumpkin puree
- ½ cup apples, chopped fine
- 1 ¼ cups steel cut oats
- ½ tsp cinnamon
- ¼ tsp nutmeg

Directions:
1. Place all ingredients in crock pot and stir to combine.
2. Add the lid and cook on low heat for 6 hours, or high heat for 3 hours, stirring occasionally.
3. stir well before serving.
- **Nutrition Facts:** Per Serving: Calories 223, total Carbs 41g, net Carbs 34g, Fiber 7g, Protein 9g, Fat 3g, saturated Fat 1g, sugar 5g, sodium 4mg, Cholesterol 0mg

2.   Turkey & Spinach Breakfast Bake

Servings: 6
Cooking Time: 4 Hours
Ingredients:
- nonstick cooking spray
- 10 eggs
- 1 cup spinach, chopped
- 1 cup lean turkey, chopped
- 1 cup red peppers, diced
- 1 cup onion, diced
- 1 tsp garlic powder
- ½ tsp onion powder
- ¼ tsp salt
- ¼ tsp pepper

Directions:
1. spray crock pot with cooking spray.
2. In a large bowl, beat eggs. stir in the remaining ingredients until combined.
3. Pour into the crock pot, cover and cook on high heat 4 hours, or until eggs are set.
4. Let cool 5 minutes before serving.
- **Nutrition Facts:** Per Serving: Calories 184, total Carbs 4g, net Carbs 3g, Fiber 1g, Protein 21g, Fat 9g, saturated Fat 3g, sugar 2g, sodium 247mg, Cholesterol 317mg

3.   Apple Cinnamon Oatmeal

Servings:4
Cooking Time: 8 Hours
Ingredients:
- 2 peeled and sliced apples
- 1 tbsp cinnamon
- ⅓ Cup brown sugar
- 2 cups rolled oats, old-fashioned
- Pinch of salt
- 4 cups water

Directions:
1. Place the apples in the crockpot bottom then add cinnamon and sugar over the apples. Stir to mix.
2. Add the oats over apples evenly then add salt and water. Do not stir.
3. Cover and cook for about 8-9 hours on low or cook overnight.
4. Stir well, making sure oats are not at the bottom.
5. Serve.
- **Nutrition Facts:** Per Serving: Calories: 232.4, total fat: 3.1g, saturated fat: 1g, total carbs: 53g, net carbs: 47g, protein: 5.2g, sugars: 20.9g, fiber: 6g, sodium: 4.9mg, potassium: 263mg

4.   Tangy Lemon Cornmeal Bread

Servings: 2
Cooking Time: 2 Hours
Ingredients:
- 1 cup of All Purpose Flour
- ¼ of a cup of Yellow Cornmeal
- 1 tbsp of Poppy Seeds
- 1 tbsp of granulated Raw Sugar
- 1 tbsp of Unsalted Butter
- 1 Large Fresh Egg
- 1/4 of a cup of Milk
- 1 tbsp of Lemon Zest (finely shredded Lemon Peel)
- 1 tbsp of fresh Lemon Juice
- 1 tsp of Baking Powder
- 1/8 of a tsp of Sea Salt

Directions:
1. Lightly oil the inside surface of your crockpot liner/bowl
2. Whisk or sift together the flour, cornmeal, salt, poppy seed and baking powder to aerate and thoroughly combine it
3. Whisk together the milk, eggs, butter, sugar, lemon zest and juice in another bowl to thoroughly combine
4. Gently, without over mixing, combine the wet ingredients into the flour mixture
5. Then carefully pour or spoon the batter into your oiled slow cooker
6. Cook the bread covered for 90 minutes to 2 hours on high. Test it by inserting a wooden skewer into the center, when it comes out clean it's cooked
7. Remove the ceramic cooking bowl and let it cool for 15 minutes, before loosen the edges with a spatula, then remove the bread to a cooling rack until completely cooled
8. Glaze the bread with a mixture of 1 tsp of fresh lemon juice and ½ a tsp of fresh lemon or lime zest mixed in ½ a cup of fresh yoghurt and ½ a cup of cream cheese
- **Nutrition Facts:** Per Serving:220cal, 8g fat, 4g saturated fat, 50mg chol, 23omg Sodium, 33g Carb, 1g fiber

5.   Amazing Overnight Apple And Cinnamon Oatmeal

Servings:2
Cooking Time: 7 Hours
Ingredients:
- ¾ cup coconut milk
- 1 diced whole apple
- ½ cup steel cut oats
- ½ tbsp raw honey
- 1 tbsp coconut oil
- ¾ cup water, fresh
- ¼ tbsp salt to taste, sea
- 1 tbsp cinnamon

Directions:
1. Spray your crockpot with cooking oil. This is to prevent food from sticking.
2. Add water, coconut milk, apples, oats, coconut oil, raw honey, salt, and cinnamon. Stir to combine.
3. Cover and cook for about 6-7 hours on low.
4. Serve hot with favorite toppings.
- **Nutrition Facts:** Per Serving: Calories: 284, total fat: 17.9g, saturated fat: 15g, total carbs: 30.3g, net carbs: 25.6g, protein: 4.2g, sugars: 1.3g, fiber: 4.7g, sodium: 30mg, potassium: 90mg

6.   Berry French Toast Casserole

Servings: 8
Cooking Time: 3 Hours
Ingredients:
- Butter flavored cooking spray
- 2 cups whole grain bread, cubed
- 4 egg whites
- 1 cup coconut milk
- 2 tbsp. maple syrup
- 1 tsp vanilla
- ½ tsp almond extract
- 1 tsp ground cinnamon
- 1 cup blueberries

Directions:
1. spray the crock pot with cooking spray.
2. Place the bread in an even layer on the bottom of the pot.
3. In a large bowl, whisk together egg whites, milk, syrup, vanilla, almond extract, and cinnamon.
4. Pour egg mixture over bread and stir to coat well. sprinkle blueberries over the top.
5. Add the lid and cook on low 6 hours, or high for 3 hours. the casserole is done when it passes the toothpick test. serve immediately.
- **Nutrition Facts:** Per Serving: Calories 123, total Carbs 13g, net Carbs 10g, Fiber 3g, Protein 4g, Fat 7g, saturated Fat 5g, sugar 6g, sodium 76mg, Cholesterol 0mg

7.   Cauliflower Oatmeal

Servings:1
Cooking Time: 10 Minutes
Ingredients:
- 1 cup cauliflower rice
- ½ cup almond milk, unsweetened
- 1 sliced strawberry
- ¼ tbsp stevia
- ½ tbsp cinnamon
- ½ tbsp peanut butter

Directions:
1. Place the rice in a crockpot then add milk, stevia, and cinnamon. Boil over high heat while stirring.
2. Reduce heat to low and continue to boil for about 8-10 minutes while stirring.
3. Add more milk if too thick and transfer to a bowl.
4. Drizzle the cauliflower oatmeal with peanut butter then top with strawberry slices.
5. Serve and enjoy.
- **Nutrition Facts:** Per Serving: Calories: 139, total fat: 6.6g, saturated fat: 0.8g, total carbs: 16.3g, net carbs: 9g, protein: 6.8g, sugars: 5.8g, fiber: 7.3g, sodium: 230.3g, potassium: 217.3mg

8.   Peanut Butter & Banana Oatmeal Bars

Servings: 8
Cooking Time: 4 Hours
Ingredients:
- Butter flavored cooking spray
- 1 ½ cups rolled oats
- 1/3 cup stevia
- 1 tsp baking powder
- ¾ cup almond milk
- 2 tbsp. coconut oil, melted
- 1 egg
- ½ cup peanut butter, sugar-free
- 1 tsp vanilla
- 1 banana, sliced

Directions:
1. spray the crock pot with cooking spray.
2. In a large bowl, combine oats, stevia, and baking powder.
3. stir in milk, oil, egg, peanut butter, and vanilla until thoroughly combined.
4. Press mixture, in an even layer, in the crock pot. Lay the sliced bananas over the top.
5. Add the lid and cook on low heat 6 hours, or high heat 3 hours, until edges start to brown. Let cool 10 minutes before slicing and serving.
- **Nutrition Facts:** Per Serving: Calories 295, total Carbs 35g, net Carbs 30g, Fiber 5g, Protein 9g, Fat 15g, saturated Fat 5g, sugar 11g, sodium 76mg, Cholesterol 20mg

9. Delicious Apple Blueberry Risotto

Servings: 2
Cooking Time: 8 Hours
Ingredients:
- 2 tbsp of Olive Oil
- 1 cup of Arborio rice
- 2 large Fresh Apples, cored, diced
- 1 cup of Apple juice
- 1 cup of dried Blueberries
- 1 tsp of ground Cinnamon
- 1 tsp of Sea Salt
- 2 cups of Nut or Dairy Milk

Directions:
1. Place the oil in your cooker bowl and using the sauté option, cook the rice until heated and has a nice golden color (If your crockpot does not have a sauté option, use a separate pan)
2. Cook the rice on high for 4 to 5 hours or low for 7 to 8 hours
3. Once the rice is cooked, add the blueberries and mix them well together
4. Serve this dish at room temperature
5. Garnish the dish with sliced nuts and or fresh fruit.
- **Nutrition Facts:** Per Serving:825 cal, 23.3g total fat, 6.7g sat. fat, 24mg chol, 424mg Sodium, 142.8g carb, 10.6g fiber, 15.5g Protein

10. Mouth Watering Egg Casserole

Servings: 2
Cooking Time: 10 Hours
Ingredients:
- 1oz of Prosciutto or Ham, cut into ½ inch slices
- ½ a cup of Button Mushrooms, thinly sliced
- 1 tbsp of Red Capsicum, seeded and thinly sliced
- ¼ of a cup of cooked diced Potatoes
- ¼ of a cup of frozen and chopped Spinach, thawed and drained
- ¼ of a cup of frozen Artichoke Hearts, thawed, then quartered
- 1 tbsp of Sun-dried Tomatoes, drained and then chopped up
- 1oz of Swiss Cheese, diced
- 1oz of Goat Feta Cheese
- 2 fresh Eggs
- 1 tsp of Dijon Mustard
- 1 cup of Whole Milk
- Sea Salt and freshly Cracked Black pepper to Taste
- A few fresh whole Basil Leaves for garnish

Directions:
1. Place a crockpot liner inside your 2 quart slow cooker and give it a coating of cooking oil
2. Grill the prosciutto until it becomes crisp, about 4 minutes, retain the fat
3. Sauté the capsicum and mushrooms until soft, about 4 minutes in the butter and fat
4. Place the potatoes in the base of your crockpot and on top, place half of the capsicum mushroom mixture in an even layer
5. Add half the artichoke hearts, the spinach and the sundried tomatoes in layers
6. Sprinkle on half the Swiss cheese, follow this with the remaining vegetables in layers and the remaining cheese then the feta cheese
7. Combine together the milk, eggs and mustard and pour this mixture over the vegetables to settle through the whole dish
8. Place the crisped prosciutto on top
9. Cook the bake for 8 hours on low or for 4 hours on high. Remove the casserole from the crockpot using the liner. Then rest it for about 10 minutes before removing the liner
10. Slice and serve it with the fresh basil leaves as a garnish and serve with a leafy green salad
- **Nutrition Facts:** Per Serving:297 cal, 17g total fat, 11g sat. fat, 212mg chol, 416mg Sodium, 20.8g carb, 2.4g fiber, 15.8g Protein

11. Breakfast Casserole

Servings:12
Cooking Time: 10 Hours
Ingredients:

- 32 ounces hash browns, frozen
- 1 lb cubed lean ham, cooked
- 1½ cups of cheese, shredded
- 1 cup skim milk
- 2 Onions
- 1 tbsp black pepper
- 12 eggs
- 1 tbsp salt

Directions:

1. Prepare your crockpot by spraying with cooking oil.
2. Divide the ham, potatoes, cheese, and veggies to create several layers in the crockpot of each.
3. To create layers, add hash browns, then ham, then onions, then pepper and lastly cheese. Repeat for several layers.
4. Beat eggs, pepper, salt, and milk over the layers. Cover the crockpot.
5. Cook for about 10-12 hours or overnight.
6. Serve.

- **Nutrition Facts:** Per Serving: Calories: 2228.8, total fat: 11.6g, saturated fat: 7g, total carbs: 16.6g, net carbs: 16.1g, protein: 14.7g, sugars: 1.4g, fiber: 0.5g, sodium: 735.2mg, potassium: 414.5mg

12. Tantalizing Cranberry Apple French Toast

Servings:2
Cooking Time: 5 Hours
Ingredients:

- 1 loaf of Yesterday's French Bread
- 1 large whole Apple, cut to bite size chunks
- 4 fresh Eggs
- 1/4 of a cup of dried Cranberries (or any berries)
- ¾ of a cup of Cashew or Almond Nut Milk
- ½ a cup of Coconut Cream or full Cream Milk
- 1 tbsp of Pomegranate Molasses
- 1 tbsp of Raw Honey
- 1/2 tbsp of Vanilla Extract
- ¼ of a tbsp of Cinnamon or Nutmeg

Directions:

1. Slice the bread into 1in cubes
2. Lightly oil your crockpot bowl
3. Place the apple, cranberries and bread in the crockpot and mix together
4. Whisk together the milks, eggs, honey, vanilla, pomegranate molasses and cinnamon. Then pour the egg mixture over the mixture in your crockpot and stir to mix evenly
5. Place on the lid and cook the French bread for 5 to 6 hours on low

- **Nutrition Facts:** Per Serving:402 cal, 15.1g total fat, 4.9g sat fat, 281 chol, 226mg sodium, 4.9 fiber, 14.4 Protein

13. Delectable Potato Bake

Servings: 2
Cooking Time: 8 Hours
Ingredients:
- ½lb of Potatoes, diced into 1/2in cubes
- 2oz of Canadian Bacon
- 1 diced Onion
- ½ a cup of Cheddar Cheese, shredded
- 3 tbsp of grated Parmesan
- 4 fresh Eggs
- ¼ of a cup of Fresh Milk
- 1 tbsp of Flour
- Sea Salt and White Pepper to taste

Directions:
1. Lightly oil the inside of your crockpot and layer one third of the diced potatoes on the bottom. Then place a layer of bacon, a layer of onion and a layer of cheese on top
2. Repeat with another layer each of potatoes, bacon, onion and cheese
3. Then place the final layer of potatoes, bacon, onion and cheese
4. Whisk the rest of the ingredients in a bowl and pouring them over the mixture in your crockpot
5. Place on the lid and cook for 6 to 8 hours on low
- **Nutrition Facts:** Per Serving:cal 669, total fat,40.7g, sat fat 22.6, chol 436mg, sodium 1305mg, carb 28.9g, fiber 3.9g, protein 48.8g

14. Crockpot Breakfast Casserole

Servings:8
Cooking Time: 6 Hours
Ingredients:
- 16-ounce frozen potatoes, hash brown
- ½ pound bacon, cooked and diced
- ½ cup diced mushrooms
- 2 cups milk
- 2 cups cheddar cheese, shredded
- ½ cup onion, chopped
- 10 eggs, large
- Pepper to taste
- Salt to taste

Directions:
1. Place potatoes, cheese, onion, bacon, and mushrooms in a bowl. Stir together.
2. Add pepper and salt, then place in a crockpot. Make sure the crockpot is prepared by spraying cooking oil.
3. Whisk eggs and milk together then pour over mixture in the crockpot — season with pepper and salt.
4. Cover the crockpot and cook for about 6-7 hours. Ensure the eggs are set.
5. Serve and enjoy.
- **Nutrition Facts:** Per Serving: Calories: 419 total fat: 28g saturated fat: 12.3g total carbs: 13.9g net carbs: 12.3g protein: 27.6g sugars: 4.4g fiber: 1.6g sodium: 959mg potassium: 552mg

15. Dreamy Lemon Berry Steel Cut Oats

Servings: 2
Cooking Time: 5-8 Hours
Ingredients:

- 1 cup steel-cut oats
- 1 tbsp pomegranate molasses
- 1 tbsp grated lemon zest
- 1 tbsp lemon juice
- 1 cup fresh strawberries and cranberries
- 1 tbsp olive oil
- 4 cups water
- ½ cup coconut milk
- ½ tbsp salt
- ¼ cup chia seeds

Directions:

1. Preheat your crockpot.
2. Meanwhile, sauté oil and oats, then toast in the crockpot, while stirring constantly.
3. Add water, milk, and molasses to the pot and mix together.
4. Add lemon zest, lemon juice, and salt, then stir to mix well.
5. Cover and cook for about 5-8 hours on low.
6. Add chia seeds and berries then mix well.
7. Allow the mixture to rest for a few minutes and serve with cow's cream.
- **Nutrition Facts:** Per Serving: Calories: 420, total fat: 17.5g, saturated fat: 3.3g, total carbs: 35.2g, net carbs: 24.6g, protein: 14.9g, sugars: 1.95g, fiber: 10.6g, sodium: 372mg, potassium: 161mg

16. Veggie Hash

Servings: 6
Cooking Time: 4 Hours
Ingredients:

- nonstick cooking spray
- 4 cups potatoes, cubed
- 1 cup onion, diced
- 1 red bell pepper, chopped
- 1 yellow bell pepper, chopped
- ½ lb. mushrooms, quartered
- 3 cloves garlic, diced fine
- 1 ¼ cups asparagus, chopped
- ½ tsp salt
- ½ tsp black pepper
- 1 cup vegetable broth, low sodium

Directions:

1. spray crock pot with cooking spray.
2. Place the vegetables in the crock pot and sprinkle with salt and pepper.
3. Pour the broth over the vegetables and stir to combine.
4. Add the lid and cook on high for 4 hours, or until liquid is absorbed and vegetables are done. serve immediately.
- **Nutrition Facts:** Per Serving: Calories 160, total Carbs 27g, net Carbs 23g, Fiber 4g, Protein 5g, Fat 5g, saturated Fat 1g, sugar 3g, sodium 361mg, Cholesterol 0mg

17. Apple Pecan Breakfast Pudding

Servings: 6
Cooking Time: 4 Hours
Ingredients:

- nonstick cooking spray
- 12 slices whole-wheat baguette, 1-inch thick
- 4 eggs
- ¾ cup almond milk
- 1 tbsp. stevia
- 2 tbsp. maple syrup
- 1 tbsp. vanilla
- 1 tsp cinnamon
- 1 large apple, peeled & diced
- ½ lemon, freshly squeezed
- ½ cup pecans, chopped

Directions:

1. spray the crock pot with cooking spray.
2. Place the bread sliced in an even layer on the bottom of the pot.
3. In a large bowl, whisk together eggs, milk, stevia, syrup, vanilla, and cinnamon. Pour over bread, making sure each slice is completely covered.
4. In a separate mixing bowl, combine apples and lemon juice and toss to coat. Place apples on top of the ingredients in the pot. sprinkle pecans over the top.
5. Cover and cook on low 4 hours, or on high 2 hours until the bread pudding passes the toothpick test. serve warm.
- **Nutrition Facts:** Per Serving: Calories 292, total Carbs 39g, net Carbs 36g, Fiber 3g, Protein 10g, Fat 10g, saturated Fat 2g, sugar 12g, sodium 365mg, Cholesterol 107mg

18. Wonderful Spicy Breakfast Casserole

Servings:2
Cooking Time: 8 Hours
Ingredients:

- 2 whole apples, medium and thinly sliced
- 1 cup natural muesli
- ½ tbsp Cinnamon
- 1 tbsp butter, Unsalted

Directions:

1. Place the apples in a crockpot then add all the remaining ingredients.
2. Cover the pot and cook for about 8 hours.
3. Remove and serve with pure dairy cream.
- **Nutrition Facts:** Per Serving:Calories: 218, total fat: 7g, saturated fat: 2g, total carbs: 38g, net carbs: 34g, protein: 3g, sugars: 9.5g, fiber: 4g, sodium: 15mg, potassium: 181mg

19. Flavorful Greek Egg Casserole

Servings: 2
Cooking Time: 4 Hours
Ingredients:
- 4 fresh Eggs, whisked together
- 1 cups of Baby Spinach, sliced
- 1 cup of finely sliced Button Mushrooms
- 1 small finely diced Red Onion
- ¼ of a cup of Sun-dried Tomatoes
- 1 tbsp of Nut or Dairy
- ¼ of a cup of Feta Cheese
- 1 tsp of Garlic Powder
- Freshly ground Black Pepper to taste
- Sea Salt to taste

Directions:
1. Place the eggs, milk, garlic powder, salt & pepper in a bowl and whisk them together
2. Add the onion, mushrooms and sun-dried tomatoes
3. Pour this mixture into your slow cooker and add the feta cheese
4. Place on the lid and cook on low for 4 to 6 hours
- **Nutrition Facts:** Per Serving:258 cal, 15.6g total fat, 5.3g sat fat, 496 chol, 536mg. 10g carb, 1.4g fiber, 20.2g protein

20. Mouth-watering Egg Casserole

Servings:2
Cooking Time: 10 Hours
Ingredients:
- 10oz ham, ½ -inch slices
- ½ cup thinly sliced button mushrooms
- 1 tbsp seeded red capsicum, thinly sliced
- ¼ cup thawed artichoke hearts, frozen and quartered
- Whole basil leaves, fresh
- ¼ cup diced potatoes, cooked
- 1 tbsp drained tomatoes, sun-dried and chopped up
- ¼ cup thawed and drained spinach, chopped and frozen
- 10oz diced Swiss cheese
- 10oz goat feta cheese
- 2 eggs
- 1 cup whole milk
- 1 tbsp Dijon mustard
- Sea salt to taste
- Black pepper freshly cracked to taste

Directions:
1. Place a coated crockpot liner with cooking oil inside a crockpot, 2-qt
2. Grill the ham pieces for about 4 minutes until crisp. Retain the fat.
3. Sauté mushrooms and capsicum in the fat and butter for about 4 minutes until soft.
4. Place potatoes in the crockpot base and on top, then place an even layer of mushroom-capsicum mixture.
5. Add half of artichokes, tomatoes, and spinach in layers then sprinkle with half swiss cheese, followed by remaining vegetables, then remaining cheese and feta cheese.
6. Meanwhile, combine eggs, milk, and mustard in a bowl then pour over to settle through on the dish.
7. Place ham on top.
8. Cover and cook for about 8 hours on low then use the liner to remove the casserole.
9. Rest for about 10 minutes, then remove the liner.
10. Slice the casserole and garnish with basil leaves.
11. Serve alongside with green salad, leafy.
- **Nutrition Facts:** Per Serving: Calories: 297, total fat: 17g, saturated fat: 11g, total carbs: 20.8g, net carbs: 18.4g, protein: 15.8g, sugars: 10.2g, fiber: 2.4g, sodium: 416mg, potassium: 617mg

VEGETARIAN & VEGAN RECIPES

21. Individual Egg And Vegetable Frittatas

Servings:4
Cooking Time: 5 Hours

Ingredients:
- 1 ⅓ cups corn kernels, frozen
- 1 cup kale, chopped
- 1 cup red bell pepper, chopped
- 1 cup green onion, chopped
- ¼ tbsp dried thyme
- Cooking spray
- 4 eggs
- 4 egg whites
- ¼ tbsp salt
- 1 cup water
- 2 oz cheddar cheese, reduced-fat

Directions:
1. Coat four ramekins with cooking spray and divide the kernels, kale, pepper, and green onions among the ramekins.
2. Pack the veggies by pressing using a spoon back.
3. In a mixing bowl, whisk together eggs, egg whites, salt, and thyme. Carefully pour over each ramekin.
4. Coat a paper foil with cooking spray and cover the ramekins individually.
5. Add water to the crockpot and place a trivet in place. Place the ramekins on the trivet and stack the fourth ramekin on the other ramekins.
6. Set the timer for ten minutes on high. When time elapses, remove lid and remove the ramekins from the crockpot.
7. Remove the foil from the ramekins and sprinkle with more salt and cheese. Let rest for peak flavors.
8. Serve and enjoy.
- **Nutrition Facts:** Per Serving:Calories 200, Total Fat 8g, Saturated Fat 3g, Total Carbs 15g, Net Carbs 11g, Protein 16g, Sugar 5g, Fiber 3g, Sodium 440mg, Potassium 410 mg

22. Asian Spaghetti Squash

Servings:6
Cooking Time: 7 Hours
Ingredients:
- 3 lb. spaghetti squash
- 3 tbsp soy sauce, low sodium
- 12 oz shelled edamame, frozen
- 1 cup matchstick carrots
- 1 cup water
- 2 limes
- 4 tbsp sugar
- ⅛ tbsp red pepper flakes, crushed
- 1 tbsp ginger, grated
- ½ cup green onions, chopped
- ½ fresh cilantro, chopped

Directions:
1. Use a knife to pierce the entire surface of the squash. Place the squash in the microwave to cook for two minutes.
2. Remove the squash from the microwave and cut it crosswise. Remove the seeds and the connecting strands.
3. Pour water in the crockpot and place the two squash halves on the trivet. Cover the crockpot and cook for seven minutes.
4. Meanwhile, combine soy sauce, one lime juice, sugar, pepper, and ginger in a mixing bowl. Mix until well incorporated.
5. When the time is done, remove the squash from the crockpot and place it on a cutting board.
6. Add the shelled edamame to the cooking liquid and bring it to boil. Let it boil for two minutes then drain well.
7. Run a fork around the squash outer edges to release spaghetti squash strands.
8. Divide the squash among six bowls and top with edamame, soy sauce mixture, carrots, onions, and sprinkle with cilantro.
9. Cut the remaining limes into six equal pieces and place them on each bowl.
10. Serve and enjoy.
- **Nutrition Facts:** Per Serving:Calories 180, Total Fat 8g, Saturated Fat 0.5g, Total Carbs 21g, Net Carbs 15g, Protein 10g, Sugar 9g, Fiber 6g, Sodium 320mg, Potassium 820 mg

23. Delightful Ratatouille

Servings: 2
Cooking Time: 3 Hours
Ingredients:
- 1 small Aubergine (Eggplant) cut into inch cubes
- 1 medium chopped Ripe Tomato
- 1 medium sliced Zucchini (Courgette)
- 1 small chopped Onion
- 1 small chopped Sweet Green Capsicum (Pepper)
- 1 small chopped Sweet Yellow Capsicum (Pepper)
- 1 small chopped Sweet Red Capsicum (Pepper)
- 2 tbsp of pitted Green Olives
- 2 tbsp of pitted Black Olives
- 1 tbsp of Tomato Paste
- 1 tbsp of minced Fresh Basil
- ½ tsp of Cracked Black Pepper
- 2 tsp of Olive Oil

Directions:
1. Place everything in your crockpot and cook covered on high for 4 hours or low for 7 hours
- **Nutrition Facts:** Per Serving:Al 127, total fat 7g, Sat fat 1g, Carbs 15g protein 3g, fiber4g, Sodium 488g

24. Hearty Cabbage Soup

Servings:9
Cooking Time: 1 Hour
Ingredients:
- 2 carrots, diced
- 2 celery stalks, diced
- ½ lb. turkey breakfast sausage, lean
- 40 oz chicken broth, low sodium
- 15 ½ Great northern beans
- Cooking spray
- 1 onion, diced
- ½ cabbage chopped
- 14 ½ tomato, diced
- ¼ tbsp black pepper
- ½ tbsp dried oregano

Directions:
1. Spray your crockpot with cooking spray and set to low
2. Add onion, carrots, and celery, and sauté until onions are clear.
3. Remove from pot and set aside. Add turkey sausage to the crockpot and cook on high until browned.
4. Add the onion mixture and mix well. Add all the remaining ingredients and bring to boil.
5. Cover the crockpot and simmer at low for ten minutes.
6. Serve and enjoy.
- **Nutrition Facts:** Per Serving:Calories 120, Total Fat 2.5g, Saturated Fat 1g, Total Carbs 15g, Net Carbs 10g, Protein 10g, Sugar 9g, Fiber 5g, Sodium 360mg, Potassium 550 mg

25. Almond Toffee Topped Pears

Servings:2
Cooking Time: 5 Hours
Ingredients:
- ¼ almonds, silvered
- 8 caramel-flavored hard candies, sugar-free and crushed
- 1 cinnamon stick
- 2 pears, firm
- ½ tbsp vanilla extract
- 1 pinch salt
- ¼ cup apple juice
- ¾ Cup water
- 1 tbsp light butter with canola oil

Directions:
1. Heat the crockpot until hot and add the almonds. Stir cook for four minutes. Set aside, then chop them.
2. Add the almonds in a small mixing bowl and add candies and salt.
3. Place apple juice, water, and cinnamon stick in the crockpot. Place a steamer basket in place and arrange the pears.
4. Cover the crockpot and cook for five minutes on high pressure.
5. Remove the pears from the crockpot and cut them side up.
6. Remove the cinnamon stick and boil the cooking liquid. Boil until the liquid is reduced to a quarter cup.
7. Stir in candy mixture, vanilla extract, and butter. Stir cook until the toffee melts.
8. Spoon about four tablespoons of the sauce on each pear half. Serve and enjoy.
- **Nutrition Facts:** Per Serving:Calories 130, Total Fat 5g, Saturated Fat 1g, Total Carbs 22g, Net Carbs 17g, Protein 2g, Sugar 11g, Fiber 4g, Sodium 80mg, Potassium 170 mg

26. Dreamy Kale & Cannellini Casserole With Farro

Servings: 2
Cooking Time: 6 Hours
Ingredients:
- 1 cup of Vegetable Stock or Broth
- ½ a cup of Unsalted, Fire-Roasted Tomatoes
- ½ a cup of rinsed Farro
- 1 small coarsely chopped Onion
- 1 thinly sliced medium Carrots
- 1 diced Celery Stalk
- 1 clove of crushed Garlic,
- 1/2 a tsp of crushed Red Pepper
- 1/4 of a tsp of Sea Salt
- 2 cups of coarsely chopped fresh Green Kale
- ½ a cup of Cannellini Beans, rinsed and drained
- 1 tbsp of fresh Lemon Juice
- ¼ of a cup of crumbled Feta Cheese
- A hand full of chopped fresh Basil or Parsley

Directions:
1. Place the farro, stock, tomatoes, onions, celery, carrots, garlic, crushed red pepper, and salt in your crockpot and cook, covered on high for 2 hours
2. Stir in the beans, kale and the lemon juice, then continue cooking, covered for about another hour
3. Serve with a sprinkling of parsley, cheese or fresh basil
- **Nutrition Facts:** Per Serving:Cal 274, fat 4g, chol 11mg, sodium 691mg, carb 46g, fiber 9g, protein 14g

27. Mediterranean Style Beans And Vegetables

Servings: 2
Cooking Time: 8 Hours
Ingredients:
- ½ a cup of Great Northern Beans, drained and rinsed
- ½ a cup of Red Beans, drained and rinsed
- 1 tsp of minced Garlic
- 1 small chopped Onion
- 1 thinly sliced Carrots
- 1 stick of thinly sliced Celery
- 1/2 a cup of cleaned and cut fresh Green Beans
- 1 chopped Red Chili Peppers, or to taste
- 1 tbsp of Tomato Paste
- 1 Bay Leaves
- Sea Salt to taste
- Freshly Cracked Black Pepper, to taste

Directions:
1. Place everything straight into your crockpot and cook covered on the low setting for 8 hours, or until tender. Remove the bay leaf and serve
- **Nutrition Facts:** Per Serving:195.4 cal, 0.8g total fat, 0.2g sat fat, 25.9 sodium, 37.1g carb, 10.9g fiber, 12.3 protein

28. Italian, Vegan Casserole With Quinoa

Servings:2
Cooking Time: 5 Hours
Ingredients:
- ¾ of a cup of soaked, dried Chickpeas
- 1 medium Potato
- 2 medium Carrots
- 1 small Onion
- 1 cup of cooked Quinoa
- 1 tsp of crushed Red Peppers
- 2 tsp of Paprika
- 1 tbsp of Miso
- 1 tbsp of Tamari or Soy Sauce
- 1 tbsp of Mirin
- 1 tbsp of Pomegranate Molasses
- 1 tbsp of Balsamic Vinegar
- 1 clove of crushed Garlic
- 1 tbsp of Sesame Oil
- 1 sliced Spring Onions
- ¼ of a cup of Toasted Sliced Almonds

Directions:
1. Wash and slice the carrots, onions and potatoes into bite sized pieces
2. Place everything except the quinoa spring onions and sliced almonds in your crockpot and stir to combine
3. Cook, covered, for 6 hours on high
4. Serve the casserole over the cooked quinoa garnished with sliced spring onions and almonds
- **Nutrition Facts:** Per Serving:602 cal, 11.2g total fat, 1.4g sat fat, 770mg sodium, 106g carb, 18.2g fiber, 22.5 protein

29. Amazing Vegetable Lasagna

Servings: 2
Cooking Time: 4 Hours
Ingredients:
- 3oz of baby Spinach, chopped and drained
- 1 clove of minced Garlic
- 1 tbsp of minced fresh Oregano
- ½ a cup of diced Tomatoes
- ½ a cup of Marinara Sauce
- ½ a box of Lasagna Noodles
- 6oz of Ricotta Cheese
- 1 cup of Mozzarella Cheese
- 2 tbsp of Parmesan Cheese
- ¼ of a tsp of Black Pepper
- ¼ of a tsp of Red Pepper Flakes

Directions:
1. Combine the ricotta, Parmesan, pepper, pepper flakes, garlic, oregano in one bowl
2. Combine the diced tomatoes. Marinara sauce and parsley in another bowl
3. Place a little sauce mixture on the bottom of your crockpot
4. Add a layer of noodles and half of the baby spinach
5. Add a third of the ricotta mixture and a third of the mozzarella
6. Then a layer of the tomato sauce
7. Add a layer of noodles and repeat finishing with the last of the cheeses on top
- **Nutrition Facts:** Per Serving:Cal, 350, Total fat19g, Sat fat 10g, Chol 55mg, Sodium 840mg, Carb 29g, fiber 6g Protein 19g

30. Vegetable Soup

Servings:2
Cooking Time: 5 Hours
Ingredients:
- 14 oz canned tomatoes, with no salt, added
- 2 carrots
- 1 medium parsnip, diced
- 1 red bell pepper, seeded and diced
- 1 tbsp spike seasoning
- 1 onion, diced
- 4 garlic cloves, minced
- 2 celery stalks, diced
- 6 cups vegetable broth, low sodium
- 3 cups cabbage, chopped
- ½ tbsp salt
- ¼ tbsp black pepper
- 1 sweet potato, peeled and diced

Directions:
1. Add all the ingredients in a crockpot.
2. Set the timer for five hours on high.
3. When time elapses, stir, mash the parsnips, and sweet potatoes to thicken the soup.
4. Serve and enjoy when hot.
- **Nutrition Facts:** Per Serving:Calories 135, Total Fat 0.5g, Saturated Fat 0g, Total Carbs 30g, Net Carbs 20g, Protein 4g, Sugar 14g, Fiber 7g, Sodium 250mg, Potassium 880 mg

31. Heavenly Vegan White Bean Stew

Servings:2
Cooking Time: 10 Hours
Ingredients:
- 1/2lb of White Beans
- 1 small diced Carrot
- 1 small Celery Stalk
- 1 small diced Onion
- 1 clove of minced Garlic
- 1 Bay Leaf
- ½ a tsp of dried Rosemary
- ½ a tsp of dried Thyme
- ½ a tsp of dried Oregano
- 3 to 6 cups of Fresh Drinking Water
- 1 tbsp of Sea Salt, more or less to taste
- Freshly ground White Pepper, to taste
- ½ a cup of Diced Tomatoes
- 2 or 3 cups (or more) of Green Leafy Green Vegetables (kale, chard, spinach) roughly chopped
- Couscous, polenta for serving

Directions:
1. Place the soaked beans in your crockpot, covered with the water
2. Cook, covered, for 8 to 10 hours on low
3. Then add the carrots, onion, celery, garlic, bay leaf, and dried herbs
4. Cook, covered, on low for 4 to 7
5. When the beans are tender, add the tomatoes, salt and pepper to taste
6. Add the greens about 15 minutes before serving
7. They can be served hot, warm or cold over couscous, polenta or bread
- **Nutrition Facts:** Per Serving:336, cal, 0.9g Total fat, 0.2g sat fat, 136mg sodium, 65.7g carb, 16.4g fiber, 233 g protein

32. Vegan Thai Mushroom Soup

Servings:4
Cooking Time: 45 Minutes
Ingredients:
- 8 oz Cremini mushrooms, sliced
- 15 oz chickpeas, no added salt
- 1 tbsp sriracha
- ½ tbsp cumin, ground
- 1 ½ cup lite coconut milk
- Pepper and onion blend, frozen
- 14 ½ oz tomatoes, diced
- ½ cup water
- ½ cup cilantro
- 1 tbsp ginger, fresh
- ½ tbsp salt

Directions:
1. Add mushrooms, pepper and onion blend, chickpeas, diced tomatoes, sriracha, cumin, and water in the crockpot.
2. Cover the crockpot and cook for eight minutes on high.
3. When the time elapses, remove the lid and stir in the remaining ingredients.
4. Let rest for five minutes to allow the flavors to blend.
5. Serve and enjoy when warm.
- **Nutrition Facts:** Per Serving:Calories 240, Total Fat 7g, Saturated Fat 5g, Total Carbs 7g, Net Carbs 28g, Protein 12g, Sugar 8g, Fiber 7g, Sodium 440mg, Potassium 930 mg

33. Spicy Vegetarian Chili

Servings:2
Cooking Time:4 Hours
Ingredients:
- ½ a cup of Farro
- 1 small diced Onion
- 1 clove of minced garlic
- 1 chopped Chipotle Chili in Adobo Sauce
- ½ a cup of drained Dark Red Kidney Beans
- ½ a cup of drained Light Red Kidney Beans
- ½ a cup of Tomato Sauce
- ½ a cup of Diced Tomatoes
- 2 tbsp of Chopped Green Chiles
- 1 cup of Vegetable Stock
- ½ a cup of Beer or Vegetable Broth
- 1 tsp of Chili Powder
- 1/2 tbsp of Ground Cumin
- Sea Salt to taste
- Freshly Ground Black Pepper to taste

Directions:
1. Place everything in your crockpot and cook, covered, on high for 4 hours or low for 8 hours
2. Taste it and adjust the seasoning
3. Serve garnished with extra toppings if desired
- **Nutrition Facts:** Per Serving:234 cal, 2.6g total fat, 0.3g sat fat 687mg sodium, 42.2g carb, 8.8g fiber, 12.4 protein

34. Special Olive And Feta Casserole

Servings: 2
Cooking Time: 8 Hours
Ingredients:
- 4 fresh Eggs
- 2 medium sliced boiled Potatoes
- 1 small diced Green Capsicum
- 2oz of finely sliced Portobello Mushrooms
- 2oz of Crumbled Feta
- 2oz of Colby Cheese, shredded
- 2 finely sliced Green Onions
- ¼ of a tsp of White Pepper
- ¼ of a tsp of Sea Salt
- 1 tsp of Olive Oil

Directions:
1. Oil your crockpot
2. Place a single layer of sliced potato in your crockpot
3. Spread a layer each of capsicum, mushrooms, spring onions and cheese on the potatoes. Then another layer of capsicum, mushrooms and green onions
4. Then place in another layer of hash browns, topped with another layer of mushrooms, capsicum and green onions followed by the rest of the cheeses
5. Mix the eggs, salt and pepper together and pour them over the top
6. Cook covered for 4 hours on high or 8 hours on low, then serve with additional sliced spring onions, as a garnish
- **Nutrition Facts:** Per Serving:423 cal, 30g total fat, 398mg chol, 978bsodium, 10.9g carb, 1.1g fiber, 27.7g protein

35. Exotic Curried Vegetable And Chickpea Casserole

Servings: 2
Cooking Time: 8 Hours
Ingredients:
- ½ a cup of Cauliflower, cut into bite-sized florets
- 1 small diced Onion
- 1 small diced Green Capsicum
- 1 small diced Red Capsicum
- 1 small diced Potato
- 2.5oz of Baby Spinach
- 1 tsp of grated fresh Ginger
- 1 clove of minced Garlic
- 1 cup of low-sodium Vegetable stock
- ½ a cup of drained and rinsed Chickpeas
- 1/2 a cup of diced Tomatoes with the juices
- ½ a cup of Coconut Milk
- 1 tsp of Curry Powder more or less to taste
- A dash of Cayenne Pepper or to taste
- 1 tbsp of Sea Salt, divided
- 1/4 of a tsp of freshly ground Black Pepper

Directions:
1. Place everything except the spinach and coconut milk in your crockpot and stir it to mix thoroughly
2. Cook, covered, on high for 4 hours
3. Then stir in the coconut milk
4. Add the spinach and let it wilt in the residual heat
5. Check and adjust the seasoning if necessary
6. Serve over couscous or orzo pasta
- **Nutrition Facts:** Per Serving:Cal 261, total fat 5.1g, sat fat 1g, carb 44.6g, fiber 11.5g, chol 13.1mg, sodium 978.9mg, protein 12.5g

36. Garlic, Herb And Mushroom Surprise

Servings: 2
Cooking Time: 4 Hours
Ingredients:

- 12oz of Cremini Mushrooms
- 2 cloves of minced Garlic
- 2 small mild Green Chilies
- 2 small mild Red Chillies
- ¼ of a tsp of dried Basil
- ¼ of a tsp of dried Oregano
- ¼ of a tsp of dried thyme
- 1 Bay Leaf
- ½ a cup of Vegetable Stock
- 1 tbsp of Unsalted Butter
- 1 tbsp of chopped fresh Parsley

Directions:

1. Place everything except the butter in your crockpot and cook covered on low for 4 hours
2. During the last 15 minutes of Cooking time: stir in the butter, then serve with parsley
- **Nutrition Facts:** Per Serving:Cal 120, total fat 8g, sat fat 4.5g, Chol 20mg, Sodium 450mg, carb 9g, fiber 2g, protein 6g

37. Coconut Quinoa Curry

Servings: 2
Cooking Time: 4 Hours
Ingredients:

- 1 cup of chopped Sweet Potato
- 1 cup of Broccoli Florets
- 1 small chopped Onion
- ½ a cup of drained and rinsed Chickpeas
- ½ a cup of diced Tomatoes
- 1 cup of Coconut Milk
- ¼ of a cup of Quinoa
- 1 clove of minced Garlic
- ½ a tbsp of minced Ginger
- 1 tsp of grated Turmeric
- 1 tsp of Tamari Sauc1/4 of a tsp of chili Flakes

Directions:

1. Place everything in your crockpot and stir the cook covered for 4 hours on high and serve when the sweet potatoes are tender
- **Nutrition Facts:** Per Serving:Cal 507, Total Fat 32g, Sat fat 26g, Sodium 380mg, Carb 50g, fiber 11g, protein 13g

38. Magic Whole Stuffed Squash

Servings: 2
Cooking Time: 8 Hours
Ingredients:

- 1 small ripe Winter Squash or Butter Nut Squash that fits whole in your crockpot
- 1 small diced Onion
- 1 small diced Red Capsicum (Pepper)
- 1 small diced Green Capsicum (Pepper)
- 1 small diced Carrot
- 1 stalk of diced Celery
- ½ a cup of diced tomatoes
- 1 bunch of green leafy vegetables, chopped
- ¼ of a cup of pine nuts
- 1/8 tsp of ground ginger
- 1/8 of a tsp of ground cinnamon
- 1/8 tsp of ground Coriander
- 1/8 of a tsp of ground Cumin
- Sea Salt to taste
- Black Pepper to Taste

Directions:

1. Slice the top from the pumpkin to make a lid and scoop out the seeds and stringy bits
2. Place all the ingredients inside the pumpkin and put the top back on, then place it in your crockpot and cook it covered on low for 8 hours or until soft and tender
- **Nutrition Facts:** Per Serving:Cal 231, Total fat1.3g, sat fat 0.2g, Sodium 92mg, Carb 56.5g, Fiber 10.2g, protein 6g

39. Homely Healthy Baked Beans

Servings: 2
Cooking Time: 8 Hours
Ingredients:

- 1/2lb of dry Beans, soaked overnight or for 8 hours
- 1 small diced Onion
- 1 diced stalk celery
- 2 cloves of minced Garlic
- ½ a cup of Crushed Tomatoes
- 1 cup of Water
- ¼ of a cup of Olive Oil
- ½ a tbsp of Ground Oregano
- ½ a tbsp of Ground Thyme
- 1 Bay Leaf
- 1 tbsp of Sea Salt

Directions:

1. Place everything in your crockpot and cook, covered, on low for 7-8 hours
2. Serve with feta cheese, fresh baked bread or on toast.
- **Nutrition Facts:** Per Serving:Cal 149, total fat 1.1g, sat fat 0.2g, sodium 751mg, carb 39.5g, fiber 19.4g protein 12.8g

40. Amazing Greek Gigantes In Tomato Sauce

Servings: 2
Cooking Time: 8 Hours
Ingredients:

- 1/2lb of dry Gigantes Beans, soaked overnight
- 1 peeled and chopped Onions
- 1 clove of diced Garlic
- ½ a cup of diced Tomatoes
- ¼ of a cup of Sun-dried Tomatoes
- 1 cup of Vegetable Stock
- 1 Bay Leaf
- ½ a tsp of dried Oregano
- ¼ of a tsp, of dried Thyme
- 1 pinch of Red Pepper Flakes
- Sea Salt to taste
- 1 tbsp of Extra Virgin Olive Oil
- Crusty Bread, Black Pepper, and some more Olive Oil for serving

Directions:

1. Place all the ingredients into your crockpot and cook covered for 8 hours on low or 4 hours on high
2. Taste and add salt or pepper if required
3. This dish can be a whole meal or an accompaniment
4. Garnish with freshly ground black pepper and a drizzle of olive oil

- **Nutrition Facts:** Per Serving:182 cal, 9,1g total fat, 1.6g sat fat, 2mg chol, 568 sodium, 23.4g carb 6.8g fiber, 4.7 protein

FISH & SEAFOOD RECIPES

41. Supreme Salmon

Servings:2
Cooking Time: 6 Hours
Ingredients:
- 1/2lb of Salmon Fillets
- 2 cloves of finely sliced Garlic
- 1 small finely sliced Onion
- 1 finely sliced Zucchini
- 1 finely sliced Red Capsicum
- 1 large ripe finely diced Tomato
- ½ a tsp of Garlic Powder
- ½ a tsp of Onion Powder
- ½ a tsp of Italian Seasoning
- ¼ of a tsp of freshly cracked Black Pepper
- 4 rings of sliced Lemon
- Sea Salt to taste
- 1 tbsp of Olive Oil

Directions:
1. Oil a small casserole dish with a tight fitting lid that fits inside your crockpot
2. Place the salmon fillets inside the casserole and season it with one half of the onion powder, garlic powder, Italian seasoning, pepper and salt
3. Spread the garlic, onion, zucchini, capsicum and tomato around the salmon and add the rest of the seasoning
4. Place 2 lemon rings on each piece of salmon
5. Place the lid on your casserole dish and then place it inside your crockpot with a cup of water
6. Cook covered for 6 hours on the low setting
- **Nutrition Facts:** Per Serving:Cal 225, total fat 11.8g, sat fat 1.7g, chol 52mg, sodium 59mg, 8 carb.1g, fiber 1.6g, protein 23.5g

42. Halibut Chowder

Servings: 8
Cooking Time: 4 Hours
Ingredients:
- 2 stalks celery, chopped
- 2 carrots, chopped
- 1 onion, chopped
- 2 (14 ½ oz) cans tomatoes, diced, undrained
- 2 (14 ½ oz) cans chicken broth, low sodium
- 1 tsp thyme
- ¼ tsp black pepper
- 1 lb. halibut, cut in 1-inch pieces

Directions:
1. Place the celery, carrots, and onion in the crock pot.
2. Add tomatoes, broth, thyme and pepper and stir to mix.
3. Add the lid and cook on high heat 2-3 hours or until carrots are tender.
4. Add the halibut and cook another 60 minutes, or until fish flakes easily. serve immediately.
- **Nutrition Facts:** Per Serving: Calories 125, total Carbs 10g, net Carbs 8g, Fiber 2g, Protein 12g, Fat 5g, saturated Fat 1g, sugar 5g, sodium 143mg, Cholesterol 31mg

43. Fisherman's Stew

Servings: 8
Cooking Time: 5 Hours
Ingredients:

- 1 tbsp. olive oil
- ½ lb. mushrooms, sliced
- 2 onions, sliced thin
- 4 cloves garlic, diced fine
- 28 oz. can whole tomatoes, undrained and quartered
- ½ cup dry white wine
- ½ cup clam juice
- 2 tbsp. fresh basil, chopped
- 1 tbsp. oregano
- 1 bay leaf
- ¾ tsp black pepper
- 1 lb. cod, cut in 2-inch pieces
- ½ lb. large shrimp, peel & devein
- 1 lb. little neck clams

Directions:

1. Heat oil in a large skillet over med-high heat.
2. Add mushrooms, onions, and garlic and cook 5 minutes or until vegetables start to soften. transfer to the crock pot.
3. stir in tomatoes, wine, clam juice, and seasonings. Add the lid and cook on high 3 hours, or until mixture comes to a simmer.
4. Add the fish and continue cooking 30 minutes, or until fish is almost done.
5. stir in the shrimp and clams and continue cooking until clams open and shrimp turn pink.
6. discard the bay leaf, stir well and serve.
- **Nutrition Facts:** Per Serving: Calories 121, total Carbs 9g, net Carbs 6g, Fiber 3g, Protein 18g, Fat 1g, saturated Fat 0g, sugar 4g, sodium 449mg, Cholesterol 62mg

44. Tilapia Stew With Green Peppers

Servings:4
Cooking Time: 15 Minutes
Ingredients:

- 1 green bell pepper, medium
- 1 can stewed tomatoes, with Italian seasoning
- 1 lb tilapia
- ½ tbsp seafood seasoning
- 1 cup water
- Cooking spray, nonstick

Directions:

1. Coat your crockpot with cooking spray. Add bell peppers and sauté until lightly brown.
2. Add the tomatoes then simmer until they are tender. Break down the large pieces of the tomatoes.
3. Add tilapia to the pot and stir gently. Lid the crockpot and bring to boil. Reduce heat so that the fish simmers for about three minutes.
4. Remove from heat and let sit for about ten minutes for peak flavors. Serve and enjoy.
- **Nutrition Facts:** Per Serving:Calories 150, Total Fat 2g, Saturated Fat 0.5g, Total Carbs 10g, Net Carbs 7g, Protein 24g, Sugar 6g, Fiber 2g, Sodium 350mg, Potassium 620mg

45. Delicious Tuna Mornay

Servings: 2
Cooking Time: 5 Hours
Ingredients:
- ½ a cup of Cream of Mushroom Soup
- ½ a cup of Fresh Cream
- ½ a cup of Tuna in brine (don't drain)
- 1 cup of uncooked Penne Pasta
- ¼ of a cup of frozen Peas
- ¼ of a cup of frozen Corn
- 1 diced Green Onion
- 1/3 of a cup of fresh Water
- ½ a cup of grated Tasty Cheese
- Sea Salt to taste
- Freshly cracked Black Pepper to taste

Directions:
1. Place everything except the cheese into your crockpot and stir to combine well
2. Cook covered on low for 5 hours or for 3 hours on high
3. 30 minutes before serving the Mornay, stir the cheese in
- **Nutrition Facts:** Per Serving:Cal 650, fat 30g, Sodium 790mg, carb 59g, fiber protein 4g, 38g

46. Creamy Cod & Veggie Soup

Servings: 11
Cooking Time: 5 Hours
Ingredients:
- 2 cups water, divided
- 14 oz. chicken broth, low sodium
- 2 lbs. potatoes, peel & cut in 1/2-inch pieces
- 1 onion, chopped
- 2 stalks celery, chopped
- 1 carrot, chopped
- 1 bay leaf
- 2 (12 oz) cans evaporated milk, fat-free
- 4 tbsp. butter, unsalted
- 1 lb. cod, cut in 1/2-inch pieces
- ½ tsp thyme
- ¼ tsp salt
- ¼ tsp pepper
- 1 tbsp. cornstarch

Directions:
1. Add 1 ½ cups water, broth, potatoes, onion, celery, carrot, and bay leaf to the crock pot. stir to mix.
2. Add the lid and cook on high heat 2-3 hours, or until potatoes are fork-tender.
3. stir in milk, butter, fish, thyme, salt, and pepper and continue cooking until fish flakes easily with a fork.
4. In a small bowl, whisk together the remaining water and cornstarch until smooth. Add to soup and stir to combine.
5. Cook another 20-30 minutes or until soup has thickened. discard the bay leaf and serve.
- **Nutrition Facts:** Per Serving: Calories 187, total Carbs 22g, net Carbs 20g, Fiber 2g, Protein 13g, Fat 5g, saturated Fat 2g, sugar 9g, sodium 233mg, Cholesterol 31mg

47. Seafood Gumbo Stock

Servings:8
Cooking Time: 7 Hours 30 Minutes
Ingredients:
- 1 lb shrimp shells
- 4 carrots, sliced
- ½ bunch celery, sliced
- 2 bay leaves
- 2 sprigs parsley, fresh
- 5 cups water
- 4 onions
- 3 garlic cloves, sliced
- 5 garlic cloves, whole
- 1 tbsp black pepper, ground
- 1 tbsp dried basil
- 2 tbsp dried thyme

Directions:
1. Preheat oven to 375ºF.
2. Bake the shrimps until the edges start to brown.
3. Add all the ingredients to the crockpot and bring to boil.
4. Reduce heat, lid, and set time for six hours. Replace water two to three times as needed.
5. Remove stock from the crockpot and strain. Press liquid from all shells and vegetables then discard them.
6. Return stock to the crockpot and heat until it is reduced to eight cups.
7. Serve and enjoy.
- **Nutrition Facts:** Per Serving:Calories 112, Total Fat 1.3g, Saturated Fat 0g, Total Carbs 12.1g, Net Carbs 9g, Protein 13.2g, Sugar 5g, Fiber 3.3g, Sodium 162mg, Potassium 464mg

48. Tender Galician Octopus

Servings: 2
Cooking Time: 5 Hours
Ingredients:
- 1 medium Octopus
- Sea Salt
- Fresh water
- Boiled Potatoes

Directions:
1. Remove the octopus head, discard it or use it to make stock
2. Have a large stock pot filled with boiling water
3. With the water at a rolling boil, dip the whole octopus in the water for about 15 seconds
4. This will "shock" the legs, causing them to curl up so the skin will then remain on while the octopus is cooking. Continue dipping it until the legs have curled up completely
5. Place the octopus in your crockpot
6. Cover it with fresh water and add 1 tbsp of sea salt
7. Cook it covered on the high setting for 5 hours or low for8 hours
8. To check if it is done, pierce with a skewer or fork the thick part of the leg
9. Remove from the crockpot and slice the legs thinly and serve with potato slices
- **Nutrition Facts:** Per Serving:Cal 139, total fat 1.8g, sat fat o.4g, chol 82mg, sodium 391mg, carb 3.7g, protein 25.4g

49. Heavenly Seafood Chowder

Servings: 2
Cooking Time: 5 Hours

Ingredients:
- 2 thick slices of Smoked Bacon
- 1 small diced Onion
- 1 clove of diced Garlic
- 2 cups of Chicken or Seafood Stock
- ½ a cup of Corn Kernels
- 1 stalk of sliced Celery Leaves included
- 1 large diced Potato
- 1 small diced Carrot
- ½ a cup of Raw Scallops
- ½ a cup of medium Prawns, Peeled
- ½ a cup of small Mussels, shelled
- ½ a cup of Halibut or Cod, sliced into ½ in cubes
- 1 tbsp of Tomato Paste

Directions:
1. Place everything except the seafood in your crockpot and cook covered for 3 hours
2. Then add the seafood and cook another hour
3. Serve garnished with fresh herbs
- **Nutrition Facts:** Per Serving:Cal 235, fat 6g, carb 27.9g, sodium 724mg, chol 56mg, protein 18.4g

50. Seafood Stew

Servings: 8
Cooking Time: 4 Hours
Ingredients:

- 4 tbsp. olive oil, divided
- 1 onion, diced
- 1 cup carrots, chopped
- 1 cup celery, chopped
- ¼ cup dry white wine
- ¼ tsp dill
- ¼ tsp celery seed
- ½ tsp salt
- ¼ tsp black pepper
- ¼ tsp paprika
- ¼ tsp cayenne pepper
- 3 Yukon gold potatoes, peel & dice
- 2 cups chicken broth, low sodium
- 1 cup water
- 1 tbsp. fresh thyme
- 1 lb. cod, cut in bite-sized pieces
- 20 shrimp, peel, devein & remove tails
- ¼ cup flour
- 2 cups skim milk, divided
- 2 cups skim milk, divided
- 2 tbsp. fresh parsley, chopped

Directions:

1. Heat 2 tablespoons oil in a large skillet over med-high heat.
2. Add onions, carrots, and celery and cook about 5 minutes, or until vegetables start to soften. transfer to the crock pot.
3. stir in the wine and seasonings. Add the lid and cook on high 2 hours.
4. Add the potatoes, broth, water, and thyme, making sure the potatoes are completely covered with liquid. Continue cooking another 60 minutes or until potatoes are tender.
5. Heat remaining oil in a small saucepan over medium heat.
6. slowly whisk in the flour until mixture forms a paste.
7. Whisk in ½ cup milk until mixture is smooth and thickened.
8. Add the fish, shrimp and remaining milk to the crock pot then stir in the roux. Continue cooking another 45-60 minutes or until fish is cooked through. stir in parsley and let rest 30 minutes before serving.
- **Nutrition Facts:** Per Serving: Calories 336, total Carbs 21g, net Carbs 17g, Fiber 4g, Protein 4g, Fat 3g, saturated Fat 2g, sugar 4g, sodium 626mg, Cholesterol 168mg

51. Simple Steamed Crab Legs

Servings:4
Cooking Time: 15 Minutes
Ingredients:

- 2 lb king crab legs, frozen
- 1 lemon juice
- ⅓ Cup melted butter
- 1 ½ cups water

Directions:

1. Place the trivet in the crockpot then add water. Place the crab legs on the trivet; thaw them first if they do not fit the crockpot.
2. Set the timer for ten minutes on high pressure. When time is done, remove the crab legs from the crockpot.
3. Sprinkle lemon juice on top and serve with melted butter. Enjoy.
- **Nutrition Facts:** Per Serving:Calories 199, Total Fat 16g, Saturated Fat 10g, Total Carbs 1.2g, Net Carbs 0g, Protein 12.7g, Sugar 0g, Fiber 0g, Sodium 324mg, Potassium 244mg

52. Mediterranean Chili Crab

Servings: 2
Cooking Time: 2 Hours
Ingredients:
- 1/4lb of fresh or frozen Crab Meat
- 2 whole fresh Crabs
- 1 or 2 Chili peppers, depending on how hot you like it, chopped
- 1/4 inch piece of grated fresh Ginger
- 2 cloves of chopped Garlic
- 2 chopped Spring Onions (Green Onions)
- 1 tsp of ground Dried Coriander
- 2 tsp of fresh Lime Zest
- Sea Salt to taste
- 1 teaspoon shrimp paste
- 1 cup of Cashew Milk or Coconut Cream
- 1 tbsp of Fish Sauce
- 1 or 2 fresh Lime leaves
- Fresh cracked Black Pepper to taste
- 2 tbsp of Cilantro, chopped as a garnish

Directions:
1. Blend together the ginger, garlic, chili, shallots, ground coriander, lime zest, and shrimp paste to a smooth paste
2. Place the paste with the cashew milk in your crockpot and cook covered on high for about an hour
3. Add the whole crabs, crab meat, fish sauce and lime leaves to the mixture in your crockpot and cook a further hour
4. Check the seasoning and add salt and pepper if necessary
5. Serve over quinoa with the chopped cilantro as a garnish
- **Nutrition Facts:** Per Serving:Cal 353, Fat 21, Sat fat 17g, unsat 1g, Cho 66mg, Carb 25g, Fiber4g, Protein 22g

53. Sensational Fish Slow Cooked In Grape Leaves

Servings: 2
Cooking Time: 6 Hours
Ingredients:
- 2 single serve size fillets of Fish
- 1 clove of Garlic
- 2 large Mild Chili Pepper (or hot if you like hot)
- ¼ of a cup of chopped fresh Coriander Leaves
- 2oz of fresh shredded Coconut or ½oz of Dried
- 2 tsp of fresh Lime Juice (or Lemon)
- 2 salted Anchovy fillets, rinsed and chopped
- 1 tbsp of Olive Oil
- Sea Salt to taste
- Grape leaves, Cabbage Leaves or parchment paper lined tin foil
- Several rings of fresh lemon or lime

Directions:
1. Mix together the lime juice, coriander, chili coconut, garlic, anchovies and cumin to form a paste
2. Place several inches of water with the lemon rings in the bottom of your crockpot
3. Trim the leaves so you can use them to wrap the fish
4. Spread the paste on both sides of the fish
5. Place a red chili in the center of the leaf and put the fish on top
6. Fold the leaf into a parcel
7. Place the wrapped fillets with the seam down on a stand to raise them above the liquid in your crockpot
8. Cook the parcels covered on low for 6 hours or high for 4 hours
9. Make your favorite salad to go with it and serve hot
- **Nutrition Facts:** Per Serving:Cal 809, total fat 73.6g, sat fat 59.8g, carb 36.6g, chol 14mg, sodium 536mg, fiber 18.1g, protein 12g

54. Royal Lobster Tails

Servings:2
Cooking Time: 2 Hours
Ingredients:
- ½lb of fresh Lobster tails
- ½ a cup of Water
- ½ a stick of Unsalted Butter
- ½ a tsp of Garlic Salt

Directions:
1. Place everything into your crockpot and cook covered for 2 hours on high and serve with your favorite dipping sauce or garlic butter
- **Nutrition Facts:** Per Serving:Cal 510, total fat 45.8g, sat fat 29g, chol 191mg, sodium 706mg, carb1.1g, fiber o.1g protein 24.7g

55. Creole Shrimp & Peppers

Servings: 4
Cooking Time: 4 Hours
Ingredients:
- 1 cup onion, diced
- 1 cup green bell pepper, chopped
- 1 cup celery, chopped
- 2 tbsp. fresh parsley, chopped
- 15 oz. tomato sauce, low sodium
- ½ cup water
- ½ tsp Creole seasoning
- ¾ lb. medium shrimp, peel, devein & remove tails

Directions:
1. Add vegetables to the crock pot. Pour in tomato sauce, water, and seasonings and stir to mix.
2. Add lid and cook on high heat 3-4 hours, or until vegetables are tender.
3. stir in shrimp and cook until they turn pink. serve immediately.
- **Nutrition Facts:** Per Serving: Calories 120, total Carbs 14g, net Carbs 12g, Fiber 2g, Protein 13g, Fat 1g, saturated Fat 0g, sugar 8g, sodium 561mg, Cholesterol 107mg

56. Shrimp & Sausage Pot

Servings: 6
Cooking Time: 4 Hours
Ingredients:
- 8 cups water
- ½ tbsp. seafood seasoning
- 1/8 tsp cayenne pepper
- 4 cloves garlic, chopped
- 1/2 pound turkey kielbasa sausage, cut into1-1/2-inch pieces
- 3 red potatoes, cut in quarters
- 1 onion, cut into chunks
- 2 ears corn, cut into 3-inch pieces
- 12 ounces jumbo shrimp, unpeeled

Directions:
1. stir together water, seasonings, and garlic in the crock pot.
2. Add kielbasa, potatoes, onions, and corn.
3. Add lid and cook on high heat 3-4 hours or until potatoes are fork-tender.
4. Add shrimp and continue cooking another 30 minutes, or until shrimp turn pink.
5. Ladle into bowls and serve immediately.
- **Nutrition Facts:** Per Serving: Calories 216, total Carbs 22g, net Carbs 20g, Fiber 2g, Protein 15g, Fat 8g, saturated Fat 2g, sugar 3g, sodium 967mg, Cholesterol 98mg

57. Simple Poached Salmon

Servings:4
Cooking Time: 1 Hour 20 Minutes

Ingredients:
- 1 onion, sliced1 celery rib, sliced
- 1 carrot, sliced
- 3 thyme sprigs, fresh
- 1 rosemary sprig, fresh
- 24 oz salmon fillet
- 2 cups water
- 1 cup white wine
- 2 tbsp lemon juice
- 1 bay leaf
- ½ tbsp salt
- ¼ tbsp pepper
- Lemon wedges

Directions:
1. Add all the ingredients in your crockpot except salmon and lemon wedges.
2. Place the lid and set time for forty-five minutes.
3. When time elapses, add the salmon fillets and add water until the salmon is covered.
4. Cook until the salmon easily flakes or for forty-five minutes.
5. Remove fish from cooking liquids and serve with lemon wedges. Enjoy
- **Nutrition Facts:** Per Serving:Calories 272, Total Fat 16g, Saturated Fat 3g, Total Carbs 1g, Net Carbs 0g, Protein 29g, Sugar 0g, Fiber 0g, Sodium 115mg, Potassium 320mg

58. Cajun Shrimp Chowder

Servings: 6
Cooking Time: 4 Hours
Ingredients:
- 1 tbsp. butter
- 1 onion, chopped
- 2 cloves garlic, diced fine
- 2 tbsp. flour
- 4 cups cauliflower, separated in florets
- 4 cups chicken broth, low sodium
- 3 thyme sprigs
- ½ tsp paprika
- 2 green onions, sliced
- 3 cups corn
- ¾ cups heavy cream
- 6 slices bacon, chopped
- 1 lb. shrimp, tails removed
- 2 tsp Cajun seasoning

Directions:
1. Melt butter in a large skillet over medium heat.
2. Add onion and cook until soft, about 5 minutes.
3. stir in garlic and flour and cook about 30 seconds, stirring constantly.
4. Add cauliflower, broth, thyme, paprika, and ¾ of green onions to the crock pot. stir in the garlic mixture until combined.
5. Add lid and cook on low heat 4 hours, or until cauliflower is fork-tender.
6. stir in the corn and cream until combined. Cook another 30-60 minutes.
7. Heat a large skillet over med-high heat. Add bacon and cook until crisp. transfer to a paper towel-lined plate.
8. sprinkle shrimp with Cajun seasoning and add to the skillet and cook until pink, about 2 minutes per side. transfer to plate with the bacon.
9. When the chowder is done, stir in the shrimp. Ladle chowder into bowls and top with crumbled bacon and remaining green onions.
- **Nutrition Facts:** Per Serving: Calories 338, total Carbs 24g, net Carbs 20g, Fiber 4g, Protein 25g, Fat 18g, saturated Fat 4g, sugar 10g, sodium 1010mg, Cholesterol 141mg

59. Succulent Salmon With Caramelized Onions

Servings:4
Cooking Time: 20 Minutes
Ingredients:
- 1 lb salmon
- ½ sweet onion
- ¼ tbsp ginger, ground
- ¼ tbsp dried dill
- ½ lemon, sliced
- 1 tbsp olive oil
- ¼ salt
- ⅛ tbsp pepper

Directions:
1. Cut salmon into desired pieces, and that will fit into the crockpot.
2. Place the onions at the bottom of the crockpot. Foil each salmon piece in a different paper foil enough to be folded like a packet.
3. Sprinkle spices over the salmon pieces and top with lemon. Fold the paper foil into packets and stack them on the onions.
4. Set the timer for six hours on low. When the time elapses, remove the salmon from packets and top with onions.
5. Serve and enjoy.
- **Nutrition Facts:** Per Serving:Calories 215, Total Fat 11g, Saturated Fat 2g, Total Carbs 7g, Net Carbs 5g, Protein 24g, Sugar 3g, Fiber 2g, Sodium 200mg, Potassium 520mg

60. Sophia Homemade Crockpot Seafood Stock

Servings:10
Cooking Time: 4 Hours 20 Minutes
Ingredients:
- 4 carrots, coarsely chopped
- 1 bunch celery, coarsely chopped
- 2 green bell peppers, coarsely chopped
- ½ lb fish parts, bones and tail + 2 fish heads
- 2 cups clam juice
- 1 tbsp olive oil
- 2 onions, coarsely chopped
- 1 bunch cilantro, fresh
- ½ bunch oregano, fresh
- 2 bay leaves
- 1 ½ bottles water
- 1 tbsp whole black peppercorns

Directions:
1. Heat olive oil in your crockpot. Stir cook onions for five minutes then add carrots, celery, and peppers.
2. Sauté for five more minutes, then add the spices. Sauté for two additional minutes.
3. Add water, fish parts and heads, clam juice, and peppercorns to the crockpot.
4. Bring mixture to boil then cook on low for four hours. Turn off the heat and let rest for thirty minutes.
5. Strain the stock using a fine mesh strainer so that all fish bones are removed.
6. Serve and enjoy.
- **Nutrition Facts:** Per Serving:Calories 55, Total Fat 1.7g, Saturated Fat 0g, Total Carbs 9.2g, Net Carbs 6.4g, Protein 1.6g, Sugar 4g, Fiber 2.8g, Sodium 182mg, Potassium 446mg

61. Spicy Halibut Stew

Servings: 6
Cooking Time: 8 Hours
Ingredients:
- 1 red bell pepper, chopped
- 1 onion, chopped
- 2 carrots, sliced thin
- 1 large potato, peel & cut in 1-inch pieces
- 1 ½ cups chicken broth, low sodium
- Juice from 1 lime
- 2 cloves garlic, diced
- ½ teaspoon black pepper
- ½ tsp salt
- 1 tsp chili powder
- ¼ cup + 2 tbsp. cilantro, chopped
- ½ tsp cumin
- ½ tsp red pepper flakes
- 1 lb. halibut, cut in bite-size pieces

Directions:
1. Combine all ingredients, except halibut and the 2 tablespoons cilantro in the crock pot.
2. Add lid and cook on low heat 7 hours.
3. Add halibut and cook another 30-60 minutes or until fish flakes easily.
4. Ladle into bowls, garnish with more cilantro and serve.
- **Nutrition Facts:** Per Serving: Calories 148, total Carbs 12g, net Carbs 10g, Fiber 2g, Protein 18g, Fat 2g, saturated Fat 1g, sugar 4g, sodium 296mg, Cholesterol 46mg

62. Lemon Pepper Salmon

Servings:4
Cooking Time: 10 Minutes
Ingredients:
- 1 lb salmon fillet with skin
- 3 tbsp ghee
- ½ lemon, thinly sliced
- ¾ cups water
- 2 sprigs basil
- ¼ tbsp salt
- ½ tbsp pepper
- 1 zucchini, julienned
- 1 red bell pepper, julienned
- 1 carrot, julienned

Directions:
1. Pour water and all the herbs in your crockpot. Place the steamer basket.
2. Place the salmon fillet on the steamer basket with the skin side down.
3. Drizzle ghee and season with salt and pepper. Cover the salmon fillets with lemon slices.
4. Lid the crockpot and set time for three minutes. Carefully remove the steamer basket from the crockpot and discard the herbs.
5. Add the vegetables and let them cook for two minutes.
6. Serve the salmon with veggies and enjoy.
- **Nutrition Facts:** Per Serving:Calories 296, Total Fat 15g, Saturated Fat 4g, Total Carbs 8g, Net Carbs 5g, Protein 31g, Sugar 4g, Fiber 2g, Sodium 284mg, Potassium 1084mg

63. Stunning Seafood Casserole

Servings: 2
Cooking Time: 5.5 Hours
Ingredients:
- ½ a cup of diced tomatoes
- 1 small diced Onion
- 1 chopped stalk of Celery
- ¼lb of cubed Haddock Fillets
- 1/4lb raw Shrimp, peeled and deveined
- 6oz can of Chopped Clams, drained
- 6oz Crabmeat, drained
- 40z Clam Juice
- ¼ of a cup of Dry White Wine
- 2oz Tomato Paste
- 2 cloves of crushed Garlic
- 1 tsp of Italian Seasoning
- 1 Bay Leaf
- 1 tbsp of fresh minced Parsley

Directions:
1. Place everything except the haddock, clams, shrimp and crabmeat in your crockpot and cook covered on low for 5 hours
2. Add the haddock, clams, shrimp and crabmeat and cook, covered another 30 minutes
3. Take out the bay leaf and add the parsley then serve
- **Nutrition Facts:** Per Serving:Cal 236, Fat 1g, Chol 36mg, Sodium 1789mg, Carb31g, fiber 4g, Protein 22g

64. 10-minute Crockpot Salmon

Servings:4
Cooking Time: 5minutes
Ingredients:
- 3 lemon
- 4 salmon fillets
- 1 bunch fresh dill weed
- ¾ cup water
- 1 tbsp butter, unsalted
- ¼ tbsp salt
- ¼ tbsp ground black pepper

Directions:
1. Add a quarter cup lemon juice with three quarter cup water to the crockpot.
2. Place a steamer basket in place and place the salmon fillets on top.
3. Sprinkle dill weed and place a lemon slice on each salmon fillet.
4. Lid the crockpot and set time for five minutes. Remove the salmon from the crockpot and serve with butter, more dill, and lemon, salt, and pepper to taste. Enjoy.
- **Nutrition Facts:** Per Serving:Calories 441, Total Fat 30g, Saturated Fat 9g, Total Carbs 12g, Net Carbs 8g, Protein 36g, Sugar 3g, Fiber 4g, Sodium 402mg, Potassium 426mg

65. Rich Crab, Spinach And Egg Casserole

Servings:2
Cooking Time: 10 Minutes
Ingredients:
- 2 Fresh Eggs
- ½ a cup of full Cream
- A 6oz can of Crabmeat, drained
- 3oz of frozen and chopped Spinach, thawed and then squeezed dry
- ¼ of a cup of dry Breadcrumbs
- 1oz of your favorite tasty, shredded, Italian Cheese
- Sea Salt to taste
- Freshly ground Black Pepper to taste
- ¼ of a tsp of freshly ground Nutmeg
- 1 Celery Stalk including Leaves, chopped
- ¼ of a cup of diced Onion
- ¼ of a cup of diced Red Capsicum
- 1 medium sized fresh diced Mushroom
- 1 tbsp of Olive Oil

Directions:
1. Whisk the eggs and cream together
2. Stir in the crab, spinach, bread crumbs, cheese and nutmeg
3. Season it with salt and pepper and set it aside
4. Sauté the onion, capsicum and mushrooms until tender
5. Combine everything and place it in your crockpot
6. Cook covered on high for 3 to 4 hours or low 5 to 6 hours
- **Nutrition Facts:** Per Serving:Cal 163, fat 9g, sat fat 5g, carb 8g, chol 141mg, sodium 265mg, fiber 1g, protein 10g

66. Exquisite Stuffed Squid

Servings: 2
Cooking Time: 5 Hours

Ingredients:

- 1/2lb of Ripe Tomatoes
- 1 small finely chopped Onion
- 1 clove of crushed Garlic
- 1 medium Red Chili, seeded and finely diced
- 2oz of Dry White Wine
- 1tbsp of Tomato Purée
- 1 fresh or dried Bay Leaves
- ½ a tsp of Fennel Seeds, crushed
- 10.oz of Squid tubes, cut into rings
- 1oz of Green olives, pitted
- The zest of ½ a Lemon
- Olive Oil as Needed
- Flat Leaf Parsley, roughly chopped for garnish

Directions:

1. Puree the tomatoes, then strain them to remove the seeds and skins
2. Sautee the onions until tender
3. Add the tomatoes, tomato purée, bay leaves and fennel seeds
4. Place this mixture with the squid in your crockpot, cook covered for 3 hours on low. Then add the olives, and cook with the lid off to reduce the sauce for 2 hours
5. When the squid is tender, stir in the parsley and lemon zest just and serve with toasted ciabatta or cooked pasta

- **Nutrition Facts:** Per Serving:Cal 284, total fat 8.5g, sat fat 1.5g. sodium 1855mg, carb 11.5g. fiber 4.6 g, protein 33.3g

67. Lovely Poached Whole Snapper With Fennel And Pernod

Servings: 2
Cooking Time: 8 Hours
Ingredients:
- 2 plate sized whole Snapper, with the gills, gut and scales removed
- 1 head of Fennel
- 2 sprigs of Thyme
- 2 sprigs of Oregano
- 1 lemon, thinly sliced
- 2 tbsp of Extra-Virgin Olive Oil
- Sea Salt to taste
- Freshly cracked Black Pepper as needed
- 1/2 a cup of fresh Water
- The juice of 1 fresh Lemon
- 1 tbsp of Pernod or Ouzo
- The leaves from the fresh Fennel
- 3 tbsp of Unsalted Butter
- Sea Salt to taste
- Freshly cracked Black Pepper

Directions:
1. Season the fish inside, using salt and pepper
2. Place half the tender green fennel heads and a sprig of thyme and oregano inside each fish and slice the fennel bulb
3. Place ½ a cup of water into the crockpot
4. Make 3 slices diagonally down to the bone on each side of each fish and place a slice of lemon in each cut
5. Brush each fish with olive oil and season it with sea salt and pepper
6. Place the fish on a stand in your crockpot with the sliced fennel bulb
7. Cook covered on high for 3 hours or low for 5 hours or until the fish flesh becomes opaque
8. Remove the fish with the stand and let it rest while you make the sauce
9. Place the lemon juice and Pernod in a saucepan with the liquid from the crockpot and simmer this to reduce it by about one third then turn off the heat
10. Chop the remaining fennel leaves finely
11. The sauce should have cooled slightly so whisk in the six tbsp of butter and then add the fennel leaves
12. Taste and adjust the seasoning if necessary
13. Serve the fish with the Pernod sauce and fennel
- **Nutrition Facts:** Per Serving:Cal 649, total fat 51.1g, sat fat 1.1g, chol 60mg, sodium 137mg, carb 11.3g, fiber 4.9g, protein 35.1g

68. Greek Cod With Olives And Tomatoes

Servings:2
Cooking Time: 4 Hours
Ingredients:
- ½lb of fresh Cod Fillets
- ½ a cup of diced Tomatoes
- 2 tbsp of Kalamata Olives
- ¼ of a cup of Dry White Wine
- 1 tbsp of Olive Oil
- 1 clove of minced Garlic
- ¼ of a tsp of dried Oregano
- ¼ a tsp of Fennel Seeds, lightly crushed
- 1/8 of a tsp of crushed Red Pepper

Directions:
1. Sauté the garlic, fennel seed, red pepper and oregano until fragrant in the oil
2. Add the wine, olives and tomatoes and cook in your crockpot, covered, for 1 hour on high or 3 hours on low
3. Add the cod fillets and cook about another hour or until the fish is tender and flakes easily with a fork
4. Serve the cod on quinoa and pour the sauce from your crockpot over the top
- **Nutrition Facts:** Per Serving:Cal 528, total fat 29.8g, sat fat 5.4g, chol 58mg, sodium 1214mg, carb 39.6g, fiber 4.4g, protein 26.7g

69. Magical Coconut Cilantro Currie Shrimp

Servings: 2
Cooking Time: 2 Hours
Ingredients:
- ½lb of Raw Shrimp, peeled and deveined
- 15oz of Coconut Milk
- 7.5oz of Fresh Water
- 1 tbsp of Red Curry Paste
- 1 tsp of Lemon-Garlic Seasoning
- ¼ of a cup of chopped Cilantro

Directions:
1. Place everything except the shrimp in your crockpot and cook covered on high for 2 hours
2. Add the shrimp and cook another 30 minutes
3. Garnish with the Cilantro and serve
- **Nutrition Facts:** Per Serving:Cal 529, total fat53g, Chol 16mg, Sodium447g, Carb14g, Fiber4.8g Protein 6.7g

70. Mediterranean Calamari Stew

Servings: 2
Cooking Time: 4 Hours

Ingredients:

- 1/2lb of Calamari Tubes
- 1 small diced Onions
- 1 clove of minced Garlic
- 1 Chili Pepper
- 1 tbsp of Capers
- 6 large Black Olives
- 2 tbsp of Tomato Paste
- ½ a cup of Diced Tomatoes
- 3 sprigs of fresh Thyme
- 1 Bay Leaf
- Sea Salt to taste
- Freshly cracked Black Pepper to taste
- 1 tbsp of Olive Oil

Directions:

1. Cut the calamari tubes to about 1/8th inch thick
2. Place the onions, thyme sprigs, bay leaves, chili, tomato paste, tomatoes, and garlic in your crockpot
3. Cook covered on high for 2.5 hours or low for 4 hours
4. Dice the capers, finely and slice the olives into rings and add them with the calamari to your crockpot, then add these to your slow cooker with the calamari rings
5. Cook covered on high another hour, then remove the bay leaves and thyme
6. Taste and then serve
- **Nutrition Facts:** Per Serving:Cal 430, total fat 21.4g, sat fat 3.3g, chol 528mg, sodium 809mg, fiber 4.4g, protein 38.8g

BEEF, PORK & LAMB RECIPES

71. Quinoa Enchilada Bake

Servings: 2
Cooking Time: 4 Hours
Ingredients:
- ½lb of lean ground Beef
- 1 small diced Green Capsicum
- 1 small diced Onion
- 1 clove of minced Garlic
- ¼ of a cup of Quinoa
- ½ a cup of cooked Black Beans
- ¼ of a cup of cooked Yellow Corn
- 1 cup of Vegetable Stock or Broth
- ½ a cup of diced Tomatoes with Green Chilies
- ½ a cup of Tomato Sauce
- 1 tbsp of Chili Powder or to taste
- 1 tsp of Cumin

Directions:
1. Place everything except the black beans and corn in your crockpot and stir to evenly mix, then cook covered on high for 3.75 hours, then add the beans and corn and cook 15 minutes more
2. Serve over chopped green leafy vegetables or in a corn tortilla
- **Nutrition Facts:** Per Serving:Cal 150g, Fat 5g, Sodium 280mg, Carb15g Fiber 3g, Protein 13g

72. Beef And Tomato Lasagna

Servings: 2
Cooking Time: 6 Hours
Ingredients:
- ¼lb of Lean Ground Beef
- 1 small chopped Onion
- 1 clove of chopped Garlic
- ½ a cup of Tomato Salsa
- ½ a cup of Tomato Paste
- ½ a cup of Italian Stewed Tomatoes
- ¼ of a pack of Whole Wheat Lasagna Noodles
- 6oz of Ricotta Cheese
- 2oz of grated Parmesan Cheese
- 4oz of Mozzarella Cheese
- ½ a tsp of Dried Oregano
- ½ a tbsp of Italian Seasoning
- Sea Salt to taste
- Freshly ground Black Pepper to taste

Directions:
1. Combine the beef, Italian seasoning, oregano, garlic, onions, tomato salsa, paste, stewed tomato and ¼ of a tsp of salt and bring to a simmer in a saucepan
2. Combine the cheeses in a bowl
3. Assemble the lasagna by placing a small amount of meat sauce on the bottom of your crockpot. Then add a layer of lasagna Noodles (uncooked), break them to get a good fit
4. Then add a layer of the cheese, followed by a layer of spinach
5. Add another layer of meat and then noodles, cheese, spinach, meat, followed by another layer of noodles and a final layer of cheese
6. Cook, covered, for 6 hours on low
- **Nutrition Facts:** Per Serving:Cal 516, carb 21.3g, total fat 26.2g, sat fat 15.7g, Cho 114mg, sodium 887mg fiber 2.5g, Protien 47g

Servings: 6
Cooking Time: 7 Hours

Ingredients:

- 3 tbsp. flour
- 1 ½ tbsp. extra virgin olive oil
- 1 ½ lbs. chuck roast, cubed
- 1 tsp salt
- 1 tsp black pepper
- 3 cloves garlic, diced fine
- ¼ tsp ginger
- ¼ tsp crushed red pepper flakes
- 1 tsp cumin
- 1 tsp paprika
- 1 tsp ground coriander
- ¼ tsp turmeric
- 1 onion, chopped
- 2 carrots, sliced
- 2 stalks celery, sliced
- 15 oz. tomatoes, diced
- 1 ½ cups beef broth, low sodium
- ¼ cup almonds, sliced
- 1 cup golden raisins

Directions:

1. Place flour in a shallow bowl.
2. Heat oil in a large skillet over medium heat.
3. Coat beef cubes with flour, shaking off excess, and add to skillet. Cook until brown on the outside, about 5 minutes. transfer to the crock pot, with the drippings in the pan.
4. Add remaining ingredients, except almonds and raisins and stir to mix.
5. Add the lid and cook on low heat 6-8 hours or on high 4-6 hours until beef and vegetables are tender.
6. stir in almonds and raisins and cook on high 10 minutes. serve.
- **Nutrition Facts:** Per Serving: Calories 339, total Carbs 32g, net Carbs 27g, Fiber 5g, Protein 29g, Fat 12g, saturated Fat 3g, sugar 19g, sodium 558mg, Cholesterol 73mg

74. Sassy Pot Roast

Servings:8
Cooking Time: 8 Hours
Ingredients:
- 2 pounds beef chuck roast
- 1 tbsp Worcestershire sauce
- 8 ounces tomato sauce
- 2tbsp brown sugar
- ¼ cup ketchup
- ½ tbsp pepper
- ½ tbsp salt
- 1 chopped onion, large
- ¼ cup lemon juice
- ¼ cup cider vinegar
- 2 tbsp olive oil
- ¼ cup water
- ½ tbsp mustard, ground
- ½ tbsp paprika

Directions:
1. Splash the beef with pepper and salt.
2. Add in a skillet, large, then brown the beef on all sides. Drain.
3. Transfer the beef to a crockpot then add the onions.
4. Meanwhile, combine all the remaining ingredients in a mixing bowl and pour over the beef.
5. Cover the crockpot and cook for about 8-10 hours on low. Cook until tender then skim fat.
6. Thicken cooking liquid if desired.
7. Serve.
- **Nutrition Facts:** Per Serving:Calories: 243, total fat: 12g, saturated fat: 9g, total carbs: 10g, net carbs: 9g, protein: 23g, sugars: 7g, fiber: 1g, sodium: 443mg, potassium: 802mg

75. Fabulous Chili Con Carne

Servings:2
Cooking Time: 8 Hours
Ingredients:
- 1/2lb of Ground Lean Beef
- 1 small finely chopped Onion
- ½ of a cup of Whole Kernel Corn
- 1 clove of minced Garlic
- ½ a cup of Tomato Sauce
- 2 tbsp of Tomato Paste
- 1 cup of cans of Diced Tomatoes
- ½ a cup of Chili Beans
- ½ a cup of Beef Stock
- 1 tsp of ground Cumin
- 1 tsp of Paprika
- 1 tsp of Chili Powder or more if you like it hotter
- 1 tsp of Oregano
- Sea Salt to taste
- Ground Black Pepper to taste
- 1 tbsp of Coconut Oil

Directions:
1. Place everything in your crockpot and mix it evenly, then cook, covered, on low for 8 hours
- **Nutrition Facts:** Per Serving:Cal 425, total fat 17.5g, sat fat 8.4g, chol 111mg, sodium 1528mg, carb 25.5g, fiber 6.7g, protein 42.6g

76. Shredded Green Chili Beef

Servings:12
Cooking Time: 7 Hours
Ingredients:
- 4 tbsp brown sugar, packed and divided
- 1 tbsp paprika
- 3 pounds beef chuck roast, boneless
- 28 ounces green enchilada sauce
- 2 thinly sliced and halved sweet onions, large
- 1½ tbsp salt
- 1 tbsp cayenne pepper
- 1tbsp chili powder
- 1 tbsp garlic powder
- ½ tbsp pepper
- 2 tbsp canola oil

Directions:
1. Place 3tbsp sugar and onions in a crockpot, 5-qt or 6-qt.
2. In the meantime, combine 1 tbsp sugar, paprika, salt, cayenne pepper, chili powder, garlic powder, and pepper in a mixing bowl.
3. Marinate the beef with the mixture.
4. Now heat the oil in a skillet, large, and brown the beef for about 1-2 minutes over high-medium heat on each side.
5. Transfer the beef to a crockpot and pour the sauce over.
6. Cover the crockpot and cook for about 7-9 hours on low until beef is tender.
7. Remove from the pot then shred using two forks.
8. Return to the pot to heat through.
9. Serve with potatoes if desired.
- **Nutrition Facts:** Per Serving:Calories: 278, total fat: 15g, saturated fat: 4g, total carbs: 14g, net carbs: 13g, Protein: 23g, sugars: 8g, Fiber: 1g, sodium: 658mg, potassium: 743mg

77. Healthy Hamburger Casserole

Servings: 8
Cooking Time: 4 Hours
Ingredients:
- nonstick cooking spray
- 1 lb. lean ground beef
- ½ cup red bell pepper, chopped
- 8 oz. mushrooms, sliced
- 2 (8 oz) cans tomato sauce, no salt added
- 1 tsp garlic powder
- ½ tsp black pepper
- 3 cups no-yolk egg noodles, uncooked
- 6 oz. cream cheese, reduced-fat, soft
- 1/3 cup sour cream, reduced-fat
- 2 green onions, sliced
- ¼ cup cheddar cheese, grated

Directions:
1. spray the crock pot with cooking spray.
2. In a large skillet, over medium heat, cook the beef, bell pepper, and mushrooms until beef is no longer pink. drain off fat.
3. stir in tomato sauce, seasonings, and noodles.
4. In a medium bowl, beat together cream cheese and sour cream until smooth. stir in half the green onion.
5. spoon half the beef mixture into the crock pot. top with cheese mixture then remaining beef mixture.
6. Add the lid and cook on low heat 4 hours, or on high 2 hours.
7. sprinkle the cheese over the top and cook until it melts.
8. Garnish with remaining green onions and serve.
- **Nutrition Facts:** Per Serving: Calories 250, total Carbs 24g, net Carbs 22g, Fiber 2g, Protein 20g, Fat 9g, saturated Fat 5g, sugar 6g, sodium 170mg, Cholesterol 51mg

78. Spanish Meatballs

Servings: 2
Cooking Time: 8 Hours
Ingredients:
- 1/2lb of ground Pork (or beef if preferred)
- 1 small finely chopped Onion
- ½ a cup of diced tomatoes
- 1 large beaten lightly Egg
- 1 tbsp of finely chopped fresh Parsley
- 1 tsp of ground Black Cumin
- 1 ½ tsp of Hot Smoked Paprika
- ½ a cup of Breadcrumbs
- 1 tbsp of Olive Oil
- Sea Salt to taste
- Freshly ground Black Pepper to taste

Directions:
1. Oil your crockpot
2. Place half the tomatoes and onions and all the rest of the ingredients in a bowl and mix them thoroughly together
3. Form the mixture into balls about 1 ½ inches across, you should get 12 balls
4. Place the meatballs in your crockpot with the rest of the onion and tomatoes to make a sauce
5. Cook, covered, on low for 5 hours and serve
- **Nutrition Facts:** Per Serving:524 calories, 21.8g total fat, 259mg chol, 329mg sodium, 14.6g carb, 2.1g fiber, 65.1g protein

79. Homemade Pork & Beans

Servings: 12
Cooking Time: 6 Hours
Ingredients:
- 3 lbs. pork loin chops
- 2 (15 oz) cans pinto beans, undrained
- ¼ cup molasses
- ½ cup ketchup, sugar-free
- 1 tsp garlic powder
- 1 tbsp. onion powder
- 1 tbsp. apple cider vinegar

Directions:
1. Place the pork in the crock pot.
2. Pour the beans, with their liquid, over the pork.
3. Add remaining ingredients and stir to mix.
4. Add the lid and cook on low heat 4-6 hours, or until pork begins to fall apart.
5. Remove the chops from the crock pot and cut or shred them. Return the meat to the beans, stir to combine and serve.
- **Nutrition Facts:** Per Serving: Calories 243, total Carbs 19g, net Carbs 16g, Fiber 3g, Protein 31g, Fat 5g, saturated Fat 1g, sugar 6g, sodium 557mg, Cholesterol 58mg

80. Lamb And Lentil Shepherd's Pie

Servings: 2
Cooking Time: 8 Hours
Ingredients:
- ¼lb of ground Lamb, Beef or Pork
- 1 small diced Onion
- ¼ of a cup of frozen Mixed Vegetables
- ½ a cup of Stock or Broth
- ½ a cup of diced Tomatoes
- ¼ of a cup of low fat, reduced Sodium Tomato Soup
- ¼ of a cup of rinsed and drained Brown Lentils
- 1/8 of a tsp of Red Pepper Flakes
- 1 cup of Mashed Potatoes

Directions:
1. Combine everything except the mashed potato in your crockpot and mix well
2. Spread the mashed potato over the top of the mixture
3. Cook, covered, for 8 hours and serve with your favorite chopped herbs
- **Nutrition Facts:** Per Serving:Cal 960, Fat 12.7g, chol 325mg, sodium 1119mg, Carb 44.3g, fiber 6g, protein 110.5g

81. Chipotle Steak Simmer

Servings:6
Cooking Time: 2 Hours
Ingredients:
- 1½ lb top round roast, cubed
- ½ tbsp Mexican seasoning, salt-free
- ½ tbsp Adobo sauce, from the chipotle pepper can
- 1tbsp Worcestershire sauce
- 2 cups canned tomatoes, crushed
- ¼ tbsp kosher salt
- 2 finely chopped chipotle peppers, from the can
- 1 tbsp brown sugar
- 3 tbsp olive oil
- 1½ cup red onion, 1-inch squares
- 1 tbsp finely minced garlic
- 1½ cup poblano pepper, 1-inch squares

Directions:
1. Place the roast into a bowl then season with salt and the seasoning. Mix to evenly coat and set aside.
2. Place finely chopped chipotle peppers to a bowl then add ½ tbsp adobo sauce, Worcestershire sauce, crushed tomatoes, and brown sugar. Mix to combine and set aside.
3. Add 1 tbsp olive to a hot nonstick skillet over medium heat. Add onion, garlic, and poblano peppers then spread to an even layer. Cook while occasionally stirring until crisp-tender and cooked evenly.
4. Transfer to a crockpot and return pan to heat.
5. Add 1 tbsp oil to the pan distributing evenly over the pan, then add half of seasoned roast cubes. Cook for about 1 minute on each side until browned.
6. Add the roast to the pot then stir in adobo and tomato mixture. Make sure the roast is submerged.
7. Cover the pot and cook for about 2-4 hours on low until the roast pulls apart easily with a fork.
8. Serve immediately and enjoy it.
- **Nutrition Facts:** Per Serving:Calories: 190, total fat: 6g, saturated fat: 2g, total carbs: 13g, net carbs: 11g, Protein: 26g, sugars: 7g, Fiber: 2g, sodium: 390mg, potassium: 570mg

82. Pork And Pumpkin Stew

Servings:8
Cooking Time: 4 Hours
Ingredients:

- 16 oz fat trimmed pork shoulder, 1-inch cubes
- 1/ tbsp salt-free seasoning
- 1 cup low-sodium beef broth
- 1 peeled and seeded pie pumpkin
- 4 fresh thyme sprigs
- 1 tbsp olive oil
- 2 tbsp tomato paste
- ¼ tbsp ground cinnamon
- ½ tbsp black pepper
- 1 large peeled onion
- 4 large diced celery stalks
- 3 large peeled carrots
- 4 minced garlic cloves
- 1 bay leaf
- 14 ounces rinsed and drained black beans

Directions:

1. Season the pork shoulder with seasoning and salt.
2. Add oil in a sauté pan and cook the seasoned pork for about 8 minutes until browned. Remove and set aside.
3. To the pan, add beef broth, tomato paste, and cinnamon, then whisk. This is to incorporate all brown bits on the pan bottom. Remove from heat.
4. Add liquid, browned pork and the remaining ingredients in a crockpot. Stir them to combine.
5. Cover and cook for about 3 hours 40 minutes on high.
6. Add beans, stir and cook for an additional 20 minutes. Remove bay leaf.
7. Serve and enjoy.
- **Nutrition Facts:** Per Serving:Calories: 150, total fat: 4g, saturated fat: 1g, total carbs: 15g, net carbs: 10g, protein: 14g, sugars: 4g, fiber: 5g, sodium: 170mg, potassium: 640mg

83. Lamb And Aubergine Casserole

Servings: 2
Cooking Time: 8 Hours
Ingredients:

- ½lb of Lamb Meat
- ½ a cup of diced Tomatoes
- ½ a cup of Beef Stock or Broth
- 1 small diced Onion
- 1 medium diced Carrots
- ¼ of a cup of dried Apricots
- 1 clove of minced Garlic
- 1 tsp of dried crushed Oregano
- 1 tsp of ground Turmeric
- ¼ of a tsp of ground Cinnamon
- 1 cup of Aubergine, cut in 1 inch cubes
- 2 tbsp of chopped Fresh Parsley

Directions:

1. Place everything except the aubergine in your crockpot and cook, covered, on high for 5 hours
2. Add the eggplant and cook, covered, 30 minutes longer and add the parsley just before serving
- **Nutrition Facts:** Per Serving:Cal249, total fat 10g, sat fat 3g, chol 11mg, sodium 513, Carb 27g, fiber 8g, protein 39g

84. Slow-cooked Flank Steak

Servings:6
Cooking Time: 4 Hours
Ingredients:
- 1 tbsp canola oil
- 1½ pounds flank steak
- 4 ounces green chilies, chopped
- 1¼ tbsp chili powder
- 1 tbsp garlic powder
- 1 sliced onion, large
- ⅓ Cup water
- 2 tbsp vinegar
- ½ tbsp sugar
- ½ tbsp salt
- ⅛ tbsp pepper

Directions:
1. Pour the oil in a skillet, then add steak and cook until brown. Transfer to a crockpot.
2. Now sauté the onion in the skillet for about 1 minute.
3. Add water gradually while stirring. This is to loosen brown bits out of the pan.
4. Add the rest of the ingredients then boil.
5. Pour over the browned steak.
6. Cover the crockpot then cook for about 4-5 hours on low until the steak is tender.
7. Slice the flank steak.
8. Serve with pan juices and onion.
- **Nutrition Facts:** Per Serving:Calories: 199, total fat: 11g, saturated fat: 4g, total carbs: 4g, net carbs: 3g, protein: 20g, sugars: 3g, fiber: 1g, sodium: 327mg, potassium: 756mg

85. Perfection In A Pot Roast

Servings: 2
Cooking Time: 8 Hours
Ingredients:
- 1lb Beef Rump Roast
- 1 packet of Onion Soup Mix
- Black Pepper to taste
- 2 cups of Fresh Water

Directions:
1. Place everything in your crockpot and cook, covered, on low for 8 hours
- **Nutrition Facts:** Per Serving:Cal,341, Fat 8g, Sodium 577mg, Carb.2g, Fiber 8g, Protein 32g

86. Pork Pot Roast With Tangerines

Servings: 2
Cooking Time: 8 Hours
Ingredients:
- 1/2lb of Rolled Pork Loin
- 2 segmented Tangerines
- 1 small sliced Onion
- 1 small finely diced Onion
- 1 clove of finely diced Garlic
- 1 sticks of finely diced Celery
- 1 tbsp of finely chopped fresh Oregano
- 1 finely diced Bacon Rasher
- 1 tsp of Cashew Flour

Directions:
1. Mix together the bacon, diced onion, celery, garlic and oregano and rub it all over the pork
2. Place the sliced onion evenly on the bottom of your crockpot and place the pork on top with the tangerine around the sides
3. Cook, covered, on low for 7 to 8 hours
4. 15 minutes before you want to serve the pork, remove it from the slow cooker and set it aside
5. Thicken the juices in the slow cooker with the cashew flour
6. Slice the pork and serve it with the sauce made from the juices
- **Nutrition Facts:** Per Serving:Cal 101, Total fat 4.9g, chol 11g, soduim 230mg, Carb10,2g, fiber 1.7, Protein 4.9g

87. Succulent Pork Chops And Beans

Servings: 2
Cooking Time: 8 Hours
Ingredients:
- 4 Pork Cutlets, pounded down to 1/4in
- ½ a cup of drained and rinsed Cannellini Beans
- ¼ of a cup of pitted and halved Kalamata Olives
- ¼ of a cup of Parsley Leaves
- 1 medium thinly sliced Capsicum
- 1 large thinly sliced Spring onions
- ½ a tbsp of Red Wine Vinegar
- 1 tbsp of Olive Oil
- Sea Salt to taste
- Freshly cracked Black Pepper to taste

Directions:
1. Season the pork on both sides with the salt and pepper, then place it in your cockpot with the rest of the Ingredients:
2. Cook, covered, for 5 hours on high or low for 8 hours
- **Nutrition Facts:** Per Serving:471 cal, 13.6g total fat, 3.1g sat fat, 124mg chol, 123mg Sodium, 30.4g carb, 12.2g fiber, 56g protein

88. Tuscan-style Pork Chops

Servings: 6
Cooking Time: 8 Hours
Ingredients:
- 2 tsp Italian seasoning
- 4 cloves garlic, diced fine
- ½ tsp salt
- ¼ tsp pepper
- 1 onion, chopped
- 6 bone-in pork chops,1/2-inch thick
- 2 (14 ½ oz) cans tomatoes, diced & undrained
- 2 tbsp. balsamic vinegar
- 2 zucchini, cut in 1-inch pieces
- 2 tbsp. cornstarch
- 2 tbsp. water
- 4 oz. orzo, cooked

Directions:
1. In a small bowl, combine Italian seasoning, garlic, salt, and pepper. stir to mix.
2. Place the onion in the crock pot.
3. Add half the pork chops and sprinkle with half the seasoning mixture. Repeat.
4. Pour in the tomatoes, vinegar and zucchini.
5. Add the lid and cook on low heat 8-9 hours, or on high 4 ½ hours, or until pork and vegetables are tender.
6. transfer pork and vegetables to a serving plate and keep warm.
7. In a small saucepan, over medium heat, whisk together the cornstarch and water until smooth.
8. Add the liquid from the crock pot and cook, stirring, until sauce is bubbling and thick, about 4-5 minutes.
9. top pork and vegetables with sauce and serve the orzo on the side.
- **Nutrition Facts:** Per Serving: Calories 471, total Carbs 16g, net Carbs 13g, Fiber 3g, Protein 51g, Fat 21g, saturated Fat 7g, sugar 5g, sodium 352mg, Cholesterol 159mg

89. Cauliflower & Bacon Soup

Servings: 4
Cooking Time: 5 Hours
Ingredients:
- 1 head cauliflower, chopped
- 3 cloves garlic, diced fine
- 1 onion, chopped
- 4 cups vegetable broth, low sodium
- 4 slices turkey bacon, chopped & cooked crisp

Directions:
1. Combine the cauliflower, garlic, onion, and broth in the crock pot.
2. Add the lid and cook on low heat 5 hours, or on high 3 hours.
3. Use an immersion blender and process soup until almost smooth.
4. Ladle into bowls and top with bacon, serve.
- **Nutrition Facts:** Per Serving: Calories 173, total Carbs 11g, net Carbs 8g, Fiber 3g, Protein 7g, Fat 12g, saturated Fat 4g, sugar 4g, sodium 270mg, Cholesterol 19mg

90. Kielbasa (polish Sausage) With Cabbage And Potatoes

Servings:2
Cooking Time: 8 Hours
Ingredients:
- ½lb Kielbasa, sliced into rings
- 2 cups of Green Cabbage, sliced into thin strips
- 1 small diced Potato
- 1 small finely diced Onion
- ¼ of a tsp of Caraway Seeds
- ¼ of a tsp of Sea Salt
- 6oz of Chicken Stock

Directions:
1. Place everything in your crockpot and stir to mix, then cook, covered, on low for 10 hours, then serve
- **Nutrition Facts:** Per Serving:Cal 378, Total fat, 15g, sat fat 4g, Sodium 720mg, Carb 22g Fier 5g, Protein 37g

91. Taco Casserole

Servings: 6
Cooking Time: 4 Hours
Ingredients:
- nonstick cooking spray
- 1 lb. lean ground beef
- ¼ cup onion, chopped
- 1 jalapeno, diced fine
- 1 packet taco seasoning
- ¼ cup water
- 2 oz. cream cheese
- ¼ cup salsa
- 4 eggs
- 1 tbsp. hot sauce
- ¼ cup heavy whipping cream
- ½ cup cheddar cheese, grated
- ½ cup pepper jack cheese, grated

Directions:
1. spray the crock pot with cooking spray.
2. In a large skillet, over medium heat, cook ground beef until no longer pink.
3. Add the onion and jalapeno and cook until onion is translucent. drain off the fat.
4. stir in the taco seasoning and water and simmer 5 minutes, or until most of the liquid is evaporated.
5. stir in the cream cheese and salsa and transfer to the crock pot.
6. In a medium bowl, whisk together eggs, hot sauce, and cream. Pour over the beef mixture.
7. sprinkle both cheeses over the top. Add the lid and cook on low heat 4 hours, or on high 2 hours until eggs are set and casserole is bubbly. Let cool 5 minutes before serving.
- **Nutrition Facts:** Per Serving: Calories 355, total Carbs 4g, net Carbs 3g, Fiber 1g, Protein 30g, Fat 23g, saturated Fat 11g, sugar 2g, sodium 554mg, Cholesterol 228mg

92. White Beans & Bacon

Servings: 8
Cooking Time: 8 Hours
Ingredients:

- 4 cups white beans, soak overnight, rinse & drain
- 2 ½ cups chicken broth, low sodium
- 2 tbsp. red wine vinegar
- 4 cloves garlic, diced fine
- 1 ½ tbsp. fresh basil, chopped
- 1 ½ tbsp. fresh rosemary, chopped
- 3 tbsp. fresh parsley, chopped
- ½ tsp red pepper flakes
- ½ tsp salt
- ½ tsp black pepper
- 2 cups water
- 8 slices bacon, chopped

Directions:

1. Add the beans, broth, vinegar, garlic, seasonings, and water to the crock pot. stir to mix.
2. Add the lid and cook on low heat 8 hours, or until beans are tender.
3. Heat a skillet over med-high heat and cook the bacon until crisp. transfer to a paper towel-lined plate.
4. When the beans are tender, stir in the bacon and serve.
- **Nutrition Facts:** Per Serving: Calories 248, total Carbs 25g, net Carbs 20g, Fiber 5g, Protein 13g, Fat 11g, saturated Fat 0g, sugar 1g, sodium 297mg, Cholesterol 0mg

93. Beef Provencal

Servings: 8
Cooking Time: 5 Hours
Ingredients:

- 2 tsp olive oil
- 2 lb. beef chuck roast, boneless, cut in 1-inch cubes
- 1 ½ tsp salt, divided
- ½ tsp pepper, divided
- 2 cups carrots, chopped
- 1 ½ cups onion, chopped
- 12 cloves garlic, crushed
- 1 tbsp. tomato paste
- 1 cup dry red wine
- 14 ½ oz. tomatoes, diced
- ½ cup beef broth, low sodium
- 1 tsp fresh rosemary, chopped
- 1 tsp fresh thyme, chopped
- 1 bay leaf
- 1/8 tsp cloves

Directions:

1. Heat oil in a large skillet over med-high heat.
2. sprinkle beef with ½ teaspoon salt and ¼ teaspoon pepper. Add to skillet and cook until brown on the outside. transfer beef to the crock pot.
3. Add carrot, onion, and remaining salt and pepper to the skillet. Cook, frequently stirring, until golden brown, about 4-6 minutes.
4. stir in tomato paste and cook 1 minute more. Add wine and stir to loosen up brown bits from the bottom of the pan. Bring to a boil.
5. Add the tomatoes, broth, and seasonings to the crock pot. Pour in the wine mixture and stir to combine.
6. Add the lid and cook on low heat 5-7 hours until beef is tender. discard the bay leaf and serve.
- **Nutrition Facts:** Per Serving: Calories 282, total Carbs 10g, net Carbs 8g, Fiber 2g, Protein 32g, Fat 11g, saturated Fat 4g, sugar 4g, sodium 608mg, Cholesterol 94mg

94. Balsamic Brisket With Caramelized Onions

Servings: 10
Cooking Time: 8 Hours

Ingredients:

- 3 tbsp. olive oil, divided
- 4 cups onions, sliced
- 4 cloves garlic, diced fine
- 1 tbsp. brown sugar
- 4-5 lb. beef brisket, cut in half
- 1/3 cup flour
- 1 tsp salt
- 1 tsp pepper
- ¼ cup balsamic vinegar
- 14 ½ oz. beef broth, low sodium
- 2 tbsp. tomato paste
- 2 tsp Italian seasoning
- 1 tsp Worcestershire sauce
- ½ tsp paprika
- 1 tbsp. cornstarch
- 2 tbsp. water

Directions:

1. Heat 1 tablespoon oil in a large skillet over medium heat.
2. Add onions and cook, occasionally stirring, until soft. Add garlic and brown sugar, reduce heat to med-low and cook until onions are golden brown. transfer to crock pot.
3. Place flour in a shallow dish. Coat both sides of the brisket halves and shake off excess.
4. Add remaining oil to the skillet and brown both sides of the brisket piece. sprinkle with salt and pepper and add to the crock pot.
5. Add the vinegar to the skillet and increase heat to med-high. Cook, stirring to scrape up browned bits from the bottom of the pan.
6. stir in broth, tomato paste, Italian seasoning, Worcestershire, and paprika until combined. Pour over brisket.
7. Add the lid and cook on low heat 8-10 hours until beef is tender.
8. Remove brisket to a serving plate and keep warm. Pour the cooking liquid in a saucepan and skim off the fat.
9. Bring to a boil. In a small bowl, whisk together cornstarch and water until smooth and stir into saucepan. Return to boil and cook, stirring, until thickened.
10. Cut brisket across the grain in thin slices and serve with sauce.

- **Nutrition Facts:** Per Serving: Calories 395, total Carbs 12g, net Carbs 11g, Fiber 1g, Protein 51g, Fat 16g, saturated Fat 5g, sugar 4g, sodium 445mg, Cholesterol 152mg

95. Mexican Meatloaf

Servings:8
Cooking Time: 4 Hours
Ingredients:
- 2 tbsp Worcestershire sauce
- 12 crushed saltines
- ⅛ tbsp cayenne pepper
- 2 pounds lean beef, ground
- 6 tbsp divided ketchup
- 1 tbsp paprika
- 6 minced garlic cloves
- ½ tbsp pepper
- ½ tbsp salt

Directions:
1. Cut three heavy-duty foil into 20x3-inch, then crisscross to resemble wheel spokes. Place them in a crockpot, 3-qt, on the sides and the bottom. Use cooking spray to coat the strips.
2. Combine sauce, 2 tbsp ketchup, onion, saltines, paprika, garlic, pepper, salt, and cayenne in a bowl, large.
3. Now break the beef and mix well over the mixture.
4. Shape the mixture into a round loaf then place on the strips at the center.
5. Cover the crockpot and cook for about 4-5 hours on low until no pink is seen.
6. Transfer the meatloaf to a platter. Use the strips as handles.
7. Sprinkle the remaining ketchup over the meatloaf.
8. Serve and enjoy.
- **Nutrition Facts:** Per Serving:Calories: 222, total fat: 10g, saturated fat: 4g, total carbs: 10g, net carbs: 9g, protein: 23g, sugars: 5g, fiber: 1g, sodium: 447mg, potassium: 235mg

96. Beef Salsa With Squash Noodles And Tomatoes

Servings: 2
Cooking Time: 5 Hours
Ingredients:
- 1/2lb of lean Ground Beef
- ½ a cup of crushed Tomatoes
- 1 small finely diced Onion
- 2 tsp of crushed Garlic
- 1 fresh Bay Leaf
- 1 tbsp of finely chopped Sun-Dried Tomatoes
- 2 tbsp of Roasted Red Pepper Flakes
- Sea Salt to taste
- Fresh ground Black Pepper to taste
- Chili powder to taste

Directions:
1. Place all the ingredients except the squash noodles in your crockpot and mix to combine evenly, then cook covered on high for 5 hours, Steam the squash noodles lightly and serve with the salsa
- **Nutrition Facts:** Per Serving:Cal 150, Total fat 3g, Sat fat 1g, Chol 35mg, Sodium 660mg, Carb 16g, fiber 5g Protein 16g

97. Swiss Steak

Servings: 4
Cooking Time: 6 Hours

Ingredients:

- 1 onion, sliced
- 1 carrot, sliced
- 2 tbsp. extra virgin olive oil
- 4 top round steaks
- 1 tsp salt
- ½ tsp pepper
- ½ cup flour
- 1 cup mushrooms, sliced
- ¾ cup beef broth, low sodium
- ¼ cup tomato sauce
- 1 tsp thyme
- 1 tsp paprika
- ½ cup Greek yogurt
- 2 tbsp. fresh parsley, chopped

Directions:

1. Place the onion and carrots in the crock pot.
2. Heat the oil in a large skillet over medium heat.
3. sprinkle both sides of the steaks with salt and pepper.
4. Place the flour in a shallow dish and dredge the steaks, coating both sides.
5. Cook steaks in the hot oil until brown on both sides. transfer to the crock pot.
6. Place mushrooms on top of steaks.
7. Add the broth to the skillet and whisk, scraping up brown bits. stir in tomato sauce, thyme, and paprika and pour over ingredients in the crock pot.
8. Add the lid and cook on low heat 6-8 hours, or on high 4-5 hours until steaks and vegetables are tender.
9. transfer steaks to a serving plate. stir the yogurt and parsley into cooking liquid and cook 10 minutes, or until heated through. Ladle sauce over steaks and serve.

- **Nutrition Facts:** Per Serving: Calories 483, total Carbs 23g, net Carbs 21g, Fiber 2g, Protein 43g, Fat 23g, saturated Fat 8g, sugar 6g, sodium 915mg, Cholesterol 122mg

98. Bbq Pork Chops & Peppers

Servings: 4
Cooking Time: 6 Hours
Ingredients:

- nonstick cooking spray
- 4 pork chops, boneless, 1-inch thick
- 1 ½ tsp garlic powder, divided
- ¼ tsp black pepper
- 1 red bell pepper, cut in 1/2-inch slices
- 1 onion, sliced thin
- 1 cup mushrooms, quartered
- ½ cup ketchup, sugar-free
- ¼ cup cider vinegar
- 1 tbsp. molasses
- 1 tsp paprika
- 1 tsp cayenne pepper
- 1 tsp onion powder

Directions:

1. spray a large skillet with cooking spray and heat over med-high heat.
2. sprinkle the pork with ½ teaspoon garlic and pepper. Add to the skillet and cook until brown on both sides.
3. Place the bell pepper, onion, and mushrooms in the crock pot. Place the pork chops on the vegetables.
4. In a small bowl, whisk together the remaining ingredients until smooth. Pour over the pork chops.
5. Add the lid and cook on low heat 4-6 hours, or until pork is tender. serve.
- **Nutrition Facts:** Per Serving: Calories 204, total Carbs 18g, net Carbs 16g, Fiber 2g, Protein 25g, Fat 4g, saturated Fat 1g, sugar 13g, sodium 414mg, Cholesterol 63mg

99. Flank Steak Tacos

Servings:12
Cooking Time: 6 Hours
Ingredients:

- 1¼ lb flank steak
- 1 juiced lime
- ¾ cup Pico de Gallo
- 12, 6-inch corn tortillas
- 1 tbsp garlic powder
- 2 tbsp chili powder
- 1 tbsp cumin
- ½ cup water

Directions:

1. Place the steak in a crockpot then splash with garlic powder, chili powder, and cumin.
2. Pour lime juice over the steak then water.
3. Cover the crockpot and cook for about 6 hours on low until done.
4. Shred using a fork then scoop 1½ ounces to each tortilla.
5. Top 1 tbsp Pico de Gallo to each taco.
6. Enjoy.
- **Nutrition Facts:** Per Serving:Calories: 130, total fat: 4g, saturated fat: 1.5g, total carbs: 13g, net carbs: 11g, protein: 11g, sugars: 1g, fiber: 2g, sodium: 110mg, potassium: 240mg

100.Classic Roadhouse Chili

Servings: 8
Cooking Time: 8 Hours
Ingredients:
- 1 ½ lbs. lean ground beef
- 1 sweet onion, chopped
- 2 (15 oz) cans kidney beans, drain & rinse
- 15 oz. can black beans, drain & rinse
- 14 ½ oz. tomatoes, diced
- 6 oz. tomato paste
- 2 ½ tbsp. chili powder
- ½ tsp pepper
- 1 tsp salt
- ½ tsp crushed red pepper flakes
- 1 cup tomato
- 2 ½ cups water

Directions:
1. In a large skillet over med-high heat cook beef, breaking up with a spatula, until no longer pink. drain off fat and transfer to the crock pot.
2. Add remaining ingredients and stir to mix well.
3. Add the lid and cook on low heat 6-8 hours. stir well before serving.
- **Nutrition Facts:** Per Serving: Calories 253, total Carbs 32g, net Carbs 21g, Fiber 11g, Protein 20g, Fat 6g, saturated Fat 2g, sugar 7g, sodium 671mg, Cholesterol 49mg

101.Burgundy Braised Lamb Shanks

Servings: 4
Cooking Time: 8 Hours
Ingredients:
- 4 lamb shanks
- 1 tsp salt
- 1 tsp pepper
- 2 tbsp. parsley
- 2 tsp garlic, diced fine
- ½ tsp oregano
- ½ tsp lemon zest, grated
- 1 tsp olive oil
- ½ cup onion, chopped
- 1 carrot, chopped
- 1 cup Burgundy wine
- 1 tsp beef bouillon granules

Directions:
1. sprinkle the lamb with salt and pepper and place in crock pot. sprinkle parsley, garlic, oregano, and zest over the top.
2. Heat oil in a small saucepan over medium heat. Add onion and carrot and cook 3-4 minutes or until onion starts to soften.
3. stir in wine and bouillon and bring to a boil, stirring occasionally. Pour over lamb.
4. Add the lid and cook on low heat 8 hours or until lamb is tender.
5. transfer lamb to serving plate and keep warm. Pour cooking liquid into a saucepan and skim off fat. Bring to a boil and cook until reduced by half. serve lamb topped with sauce.
- **Nutrition Facts:** Per Serving: Calories 771, total Carbs 6g, net Carbs 5g, Fiber 1g, Protein 69g, Fat 23g, saturated Fat 7g, sugar 1g, sodium 775mg, Cholesterol 369mg

102. Tantalizing Goat Curry

Servings: 2
Cooking Time: 5 Hours
Ingredients:

- ½lb of diced Goat Meat
- 1 small chopped Red Onion
- ½ a tsp of minced fresh Ginger
- 1 clove of minced Garlic
- 1 tsp of Ghee or Coconut Oil
- 1 Bay Leaf
- A pinch of ground Cloves
- A pinch of ground Cardamom
- A pinch of ground Cayenne
- 1 tsp of ground Coriander
- ¼ of a tsp of ground Cumin
- ½ a tsp of ground Turmeric
- ½ a tsp of ground Paprika
- ½ a cup of diced Tomatoes
- ¼ of a tsp of Gram Masala (or chili powder)
- Water as needed

Directions:

1. Combine and thoroughly mix everything except the diced tomatoes and gram masala
2. Cook, covered, on high for 4 hours, then add the tomatoes and gram masala, plus a little water it the curry is too thick. Continue cooking until the meat is tender
- **Nutrition Facts:** Per Serving:Cal 169, Total fat 5g, sat fat 2.7g, chol 57mg, sodium 91mg, Carb 8.6g, fiber 2.2g, protein 22.7g

103. Pork Stew

Servings: 8
Cooking Time: 5 Hours
Ingredients:

- 2 pound pork tenderloins, 2-inch pieces
- 2 carrots, ½ -inch slices
- 2 coarsely chopped celery ribs
- 1 fresh thyme sprig
- 1 fresh rosemary sprig
- ½ tbsp pepper
- 1 tbsp salt
- 1 coarsely chopped onion, medium
- 2 tbsp tomato paste
- 3 cups beef broth
- 4 minced garlic cloves
- ⅓ Cup pitted and chopped plums, dried
- 2 bay leaves

Directions:

1. Splash pepper and salt on the pork and transfer to a crockpot.
2. Add carrots, onion, and celery.
3. Meanwhile, whisk tomato paste, and beef broth in a bowl then pour over the vegetables.
4. Add garlic, plums, bay leaves, thyme, and rosemary.
5. Cover the crockpot and cook for about 5-6 hours on low until vegetables and pork are tender.
6. Discard thyme, bay leaves, and rosemary.
7. Serve with potatoes. Enjoy!
- **Nutrition Facts:** Per Serving:Calories: 177, total fat: 4g, saturated fat: 1g, total carbs: 9g, Net carbs: 8g, Protein: 24g, sugars: 4g, Fiber: 1g, sodium: 64mg, potassium: 99mg

104.Tender Sunday Roast Beef

Servings: 2
Cooking Time: 7 Hours
Ingredients:
- 1/2lb of Boneless Beef Chuck Roast
- ½ a cup of chopped Onion
- 1 clove of minced Garlic
- 1 tsp of Italian seasoning
- 1 tsp of Onion Powder
- ½ a tsp of Sea Salt
- ½ a tsp of Black Pepper
- ¼ of a cup of Red Wine or Red Wine Vinegar
- ½ a cup of diced Tomatoes

Directions:
1. Place everything in your crockpot and cook, covered, on low for 8 to 9 hours
- **Nutrition Facts:** Per Serving:Cal 121, Fat 3.2g, chol, 72mg, sodium 267mg, Protein 16g

105.Italian Meatloaf

Servings: 6
Cooking Time: 5 Hours
Ingredients:
- nonstick cooking spray
- 1/3 cup tomato sauce
- ¼ tsp oregano
- ¼ tsp basil
- ¼ tsp garlic powder
- 1 lb. lean ground beef
- ½ lb. ground pork
- ¾ cup green bell pepper, chopped
- ½ cup onion, chopped
- 2/3 cup oats
- 2 eggs
- 1/8 tsp salt
- ½ cup mozzarella cheese, grated

Directions:
1. spray the crock pot with cooking spray.
2. In a small bowl, whisk together tomato sauce, oregano, basil, and garlic powder.
3. In a large bowl, combine beef, pork, bell pepper, onion, oats, eggs, 3 tablespoons tomato sauce mixture and salt. Form mixture into a loaf shape.
4. take a sheet of foil, long enough to cover the bottom and sides of the crock pot and fold it in half, then half again. Lay it in the crock pot and spray with cooking spray.
5. Place the meatloaf on the foil sling. spread the remaining tomato sauce mixture over the top.
6. Add the lid and cook on low heat 5 hours, or on high 2 ½ hours, or until meatloaf is cooked through.
7. top with mozzarella cheese and cook just until it melts. Remove the lid and let sit 15 minutes.
8. Use the foil to lift the meatloaf out of the crock pot, slice and serve.
- **Nutrition Facts:** Per Serving: Calories 418, total Carbs 14g, net Carbs 11g, Fiber 3g, Protein 26g, Fat 28g, saturated Fat 10g, sugar 1g, sodium 276mg, Cholesterol 86mg

106. Meat Loaf Supreme

Servings: 2
Cooking Time: 8 Hours
Ingredients:
- ½lb of Ground Beef, Mutton or Pork
- ¼ of a cup of finely diced Sun-dried Tomatoes
- 1 clove of crushed Garlic
- 1 lightly beaten Egg
- 1 tbsp of Milk
- ¼ of a cup of Feta Cheese
- 1oz of Green Olives
- ¼ a cup of Breadcrumbs
- ¼ of a tsp of dried Oregano crushed
- ¼ of a tsp of Ground Black Pepper
- ¼ of a cup of Pasta Sauce

Directions:
1. Combine together the milk, eggs, oregano, pepper, garlic, tomatoes and breadcrumbs. Then add in the feta cheese and ground meat, mix everything well
2. Then place the mixture into a dish that will fit inside your crockpot and accommodate the meatloaf and sauce
3. Place the bowl in your crockpot and pour the pasta sauce over the meat loaf
4. Cook it covered for 4 hours on high or 7 to 8 hours on low
- **Nutrition Facts:** Per Serving:238 cal, 9g total fat, 4g sat fat, 74mg chol, 324mg sodium, 10g carb, 1g fiber, 29g protein 12

107. Mandarin Beef

Servings: 6
Cooking Time: 8 Hours
Ingredients:
- 1 lb. beef chuck blade steak, boneless & cut in bite-size pieces
- ½ tsp salt
- ½ tsp black pepper
- 1 carrot, diced
- 1 onion, diced
- 1 red bell pepper, cut in strips
- 2 cloves garlic, diced fine
- 1 tsp fresh ginger, grated
- 1 tsp sesame oil
- 1 tbsp. rice vinegar
- 1 tbsp. soy sauce, low sodium
- 1 can mandarin oranges
- 2 tbsp. cornstarch

Directions:
1. sprinkle beef with salt and pepper and place in crock pot.
2. Add remaining ingredients, except for oranges and cornstarch. stir to combine.
3. Add the lid and cook on low heat 6-8 hours, or until beef is tender.
4. 15 minutes before cooking time ends, whisk the cornstarch and ¼ cup liquid from the oranges together until smooth.
5. stir into the beef mixture until combined. Add the oranges. Continue cooking 15 minutes or until the mixture thickens. stir well and serve.
- **Nutrition Facts:** Per Serving: Calories 236, total Carbs 10g, net Carbs 9g, Fiber 1g, Protein 16g, Fat 15g, saturated Fat 6g, sugar 6g, sodium 220mg, Cholesterol 69mg

108.Moroccan Beef Tagine

Servings: 2
Cooking Time: 9 Hours
Ingredients:
- 1/2lb Beef Chuck Roast
- 1 small Carrot, sliced in 2 inch pieces
- ½ a cup of thinly sliced Onion
- ¼ of a cup of chopped Dates
- 2 cloves of chopped Garlic
- 1 tbsp of Unsalted Ghee or Butter
- ½ a cup of fire roasted diced Tomatoes
- 1 tbsp of Raw Honey
- ½ a tbsp of Spicy Harissa Paste
- 1 tbsp of ras el hanout
- ½ a tsp of Cinnamon
- 1 cup of uncooked Couscous
- ¼ of a cup of fresh Cilantro Leaves for Garnish
- ½ a cup of Feta Cheese, crumbled for serving

Directions:
1. Oil or spray your slow cooker bowl with non-stick spray
2. Make the couscous according to the instructions on the packet, without butter or salt
3. Place all the ingredients in your crockpot and cook, covered, for 8 to 9 hours
4. When tender Shred the beef and remove any bits of fat or hard pieces
5. Stir the shredded beef back into the sauce in your crockpot
6. Serve the Tagine spooned over the couscous and sprinkled with cilantro and the feta cheese
- **Nutrition Facts:** Per Serving:340 cal, 11g total fat, 4.5 sat fat, 55mg chol, 890g sodium, 3g carb, 3g fiber, 22g protein

109.Beef & Cabbage Stew

Servings: 6
Cooking Time: 6 Hours
Ingredients:
- 1 lb. lean ground beef
- 1 onion, chopped
- 15 oz. tomatoes, stewed
- 15 oz. tomato sauce, no added salt
- 2 cloves garlic, diced fine
- 1 tbsp. Worcestershire sauce
- 1 cup beef broth, low sodium
- 1 tsp black pepper
- ½ tsp crushed red pepper flakes
- ½ head cabbage, chopped

Directions:
1. In a large skillet over medium heat, cook beef and onions until meat is no longer pink.
2. Add the tomatoes, tomato sauce, garlic, Worcestershire, broth, and seasonings to the crock pot. stir to combine.
3. Add the beef and cabbage and mix together.
4. Add the lid and cook on low heat 5-6 hours. stir before serving.
- **Nutrition Facts:** Per Serving: Calories 242, total Carbs 14g, net Carbs 11g, Fiber 3g, Protein 17g, Fat 13g, saturated Fat 0g, sugar 6g, sodium 143mg, Cholesterol 0mg

110.Delightful Burgundy Lamb Shanks

Servings: 2
Cooking Time: 8 Hours
Ingredients:
- 2 Lamb Shanks (20 oz each)
- 1 cup of a nice drinking Burgundy
- 1 small chopped Onion
- 1 small chopped Carrot
- 1 tsp of dried Parsley
- 1 tbsp of minced Garlic
- ½ of a tsp of dried Oregano'
- ½ a tsp of grated Lemon Peel
- 1/8 of a tsp of ground Cloves
- 1 Bay Leaf
- A Sprig of Rosemary
- A Sprig of Thyme
- 1 tsp of Olive Oil
- Sea Salt to taste
- Ground Black Pepper to taste

Directions:
1. Place everything in your crockpot and cook covered on low for 8 hours
2. Take the juices from your crockpot and strain, then reduce them to a nice sauce consistency in a small saucepan
3. Serve the Lamb Shanks with the gravy and a fresh salad
- **Nutrition Facts:** Per Serving:Cal 633, fat 27g, sat fat 13g, carb 6g, chol 228mg, sodium 404mg, fiber 1g, protein 69g

POULTRY RECIPES

111.Turkey With Berry Compote

Servings:12
Cooking Time:4 Hours 20 Minutes
Ingredients:
- ½ tbsp thyme, dried
- ½ tbsp pepper
- 2 cups raspberries
- 2 cups blueberries
- 1 cup grape juice, white
- 1 tbsp salt
- ½ tbsp garlic powder
- ½ tbsp pepper
- ⅓ Cup water
- 2 peeled and chopped medium apples
- ¼ tbsp red pepper, crushed and in flakes
- ¼ tbsp ginger, ground

Directions:
1. In a bowl, mix salt, garlic powder, thyme, and pepper and rub the turkey with the mixture
2. Put the turkey on a crockpot and pour water on the turkey.
3. Cover and cook for four hours.
4. When time elapses, remove the turkey from crockpot and put it on a chopping board.
5. Cover the turkey with foil and allow it to rest for ten minutes, then slice it.
6. Combine apples, raspberries, blueberries, grape juice red pepper, and ginger in a saucepan.
7. Cook the compote ingredients as you stir until the mixture thickens, and the apple become tender for twenty minutes.
8. Serve with turkey and enjoy it.
- **Nutrition Facts:** Per Serving:Calories 215, Total Fat 1g, Saturated Fat 0g, Total Carbs 12g, Net Carbs 10g, Protein 38g, Sugar 8g, Fiber 2g, Sodium 272mg

112.Chicken With Artichokes & Red Peppers

Servings: 8
Cooking Time: 8 Hours
Ingredients:
- 12 oz. jar roasted red peppers, drain & chop
- ¾ cup chicken broth, low sodium
- 4 whole chicken breasts
- 3 cloves garlic, diced fine
- 1/4 sweet onion, diced fine
- 1 tsp salt
- ½ tsp pepper
- 4 tbsp. cream cheese, fat-free
- 4 tbsp. Parmesan cheese, grated
- 14 oz. artichoke hearts, drain & chop
- 1 cup cherry tomatoes, chopped

Directions:
1. Add red peppers, broth, and chicken to the crock pot.
2. sprinkle garlic, onion, salt, and pepper over the top.
3. Add the lid and cook on low heat 6-8 hours or on high 4-6 hours.
4. transfer chicken to serving plates.
5. Add the cream cheese, parmesan, and artichokes to the crock pot. stir until cheese has melted and sauce is creamy. spoon over chicken, top with tomatoes and serve.
- **Nutrition Facts:** Per Serving: Calories 239, total Carbs 12g, net Carbs 8g, Fiber 4g, Protein 25g, Fat 10g, saturated Fat 4g, sugar 4g, sodium 584mg, Cholesterol 62mg

113.Buffalo Chicken Chili

Servings: 6
Cooking Time: 6 Hours
Ingredients:
- 2 tbsp. olive oil
- 1 onion, diced
- 1 ½ lbs. ground chicken
- 1 cup celery, sliced
- 1 cup carrots, chopped
- 28 oz. can fire-roasted tomatoes, diced
- 15 oz. can white beans, drain & rinse
- 2 tsp chili powder
- 2 tsp cumin
- ½ tsp salt
- ½ tsp pepper
- 1 cup chicken broth, low sodium
- ¼ cup buffalo wing sauce

Directions:
1. Heat oil in a large skillet over med-high heat.
2. Add onions and cook until they soften about 5 minutes.
3. Add chicken, celery, and carrots and cook until chicken is no longer pink.
4. transfer mixture to the crock pot. Add tomatoes, beans, and seasonings.
5. Pour in broth and hot sauce and stir to mix well.
6. Add the lid and cook on low heat 5-6 hours. stir well before serving.
- **Nutrition Facts:** Per Serving: Calories 305, total Carbs 25g, net Carbs 17g, Fiber 8g, Protein 26g, Fat 12g, saturated Fat 3g, sugar 8g, sodium 873mg, Cholesterol 98mg

114.Chicken & Squash Stew

Servings: 4
Cooking Time: 4 Hours
Ingredients:
- 2 tbsp. extra virgin olive oil
- ¼ cup flour
- 1 lb. chicken breasts, cut in bite-sized pieces
- ½ tsp salt
- 1/8 tsp pepper
- 2 ½ cups chicken broth, low sodium
- 1 onion, chopped
- 2 squash, diced
- 3 fresh sage leaves, chopped

Directions:
1. Heat 1 1/2 tablespoons oil in a large skillet over medium heat.
2. Place flour in a large Ziploc bag. Add chicken and toss to coat.
3. Add the chicken to the skillet and cook until brown on the outside. season with salt and pepper.
4. Add 1 cup broth and continue cooking until the sauce begins to thicken.
5. transfer the chicken and sauce to the crock pot.
6. Add remaining oil to the skillet along with the onion. Cook about 5 minutes or until onion turns translucent. Add to the crock pot.
7. Add remaining ingredients and stir to mix.
8. Add the lid and cook on low heat 4 hours. stir before serving.
- **Nutrition Facts:** Per Serving: Calories 297, total Carbs 21g, net Carbs 17g, Fiber 4g, Protein 27g, Fat 12g, saturated Fat 2g, sugar 5g, sodium 245mg, Cholesterol 69mg

115.Capitan's Chicken

Servings: 2
Cooking Time: 6 Hours
Ingredients:
- 1lb of chicken drumsticks
- 1 small Red Capsicum sliced into strips
- 1 small yellow Capsicum sliced into strips
- 1 small Onion, sliced into thin wedges
- ¼ of a cup of Gold Raisins (Sultanas)
- 2 cloves of minced Garlic
- 1 small can of diced tomatoes with liquid
- 1 tsp of Curry Powder
- ½ tsp of Ground Cumin
- 1 tbsp of Whole-Grain Flour
- Sea salt and Black Pepper to taste

Directions:
1. Place the chicken, onion, capsicum and raisins in your crockpot
2. Combine the rest of the ingredients in a bowl, then pour this mixture over the chicken
3. Cook, covered, on high for 3 hours or low for 6 hours or until the chicken is tender
- **Nutrition Facts:** Per Serving:Cal.337, Fat89, Sat fat 2.4g, Protien45g, Carb 15g, Fiber 2.6, Chol 1206mg Sodium 442mg

116.Amazing Spicy Chicken

Servings:2
Cooking Time:7 Hours
Ingredients:
- ½lbs of Chicken Breasts or Boneless Chicken Thighs
- 1 cup of cooked Quinoa
- 1 tbsp of Tamari sauce or Coconut Aminos
- 1/4 of a cup of Rice Wine Vinegar or Apple Cider Vinegar
- 1 tbsp of Mirin or dry Sherry
- 1 tsp of Toasted Sesame Oil
- 2 cloves of minced Garlic
- 1 tsp of minced Ginger
- 1/8 of a tsp of Red Chili Flakes (optional)
- Sea Salt and freshly ground Black Pepper, to taste
- 1 tbsp of Corn Starch
- 1 tbsp of fresh Water
- For garnish: sliced green onions, sesame seeds

Directions:
1. First season the chicken liberally with sea salt and pepper, then sear it on a hot grill or pan
2. Place the breasts in your slow cooker bowl
3. Whisk together the sesame oil, tamari sauce, mirin, vinegar, ginger and garlic, then pour this mixture over the chicken
4. Cook it covered on low for 6 to 7 hours or high for 3 to 4 hours
5. Once the chicken is tender, mix the cornstarch with water and stir it in to form the sauce
6. Serve on top of the quinoa or if preferred rice
- **Nutrition Facts:** Per Serving:65 cal, total fat 6g, sat fat 2 g, 124 chol, 1271mg sodium, 53g carb, 1g fiber, 44g protein

117.Chicken Chili

Servings: 6
Cooking Time: 5 Hours
Ingredients:
- 1 ½ lbs. chicken breasts, boneless, skinless & cut in ½-inch pieces
- 1 cup onion, chopped
- 3 tbsp. olive oil
- 15 oz. cannellini beans, drain & rinse
- 14 ½ oz. tomatoes, diced, undrained
- 14 ½ oz. tomatoes with green chilies, undrained
- 1 cup corn
- 1/8 tsp salt
- 1 tsp cumin
- 1 tsp garlic, diced fine
- ½ tsp celery salt
- ½ tsp coriander
- ½ tsp black pepper

Directions:
1. Heat oil in a large skillet over medium heat. Add chicken and onion and cook, 5 minutes, or until chicken is brown on the outside. transfer to the crock pot.
2. And remaining ingredients and stir to combine.
3. Add the lid and cook on low heat 5 hours, or until chicken is cooked through.
4. serve garnished with sour cream and grated cheese if desired.
- **Nutrition Facts:** Per Serving: Calories 370, total Carbs 29g, net Carbs 24g, Fiber 5g, Protein 34g, Fat 13g, saturated Fat 3g, sugar 4g, sodium 427mg, Cholesterol 90mg

118.Greek Lemon Chicken

Servings: 4
Cooking Time: 4 Hours
Ingredients:
- 4 chicken breast, boneless & skinless
- 4 cloves garlic, diced fine
- 1 tsp salt
- 3 tsp oregano
- ¼ cup fresh lemon juice
- 1 tbsp. lemon zest
- 1 cup chicken broth, low sodium
- 3 tbsp. fresh parsley, chopped

Directions:
1. Place the chicken in the crock pot. Add remaining ingredients, except parsley, over the chicken.
2. Add the lid and cook on low heat 6 hours, or on high for 4 hours until chicken is cooked through.
3. serve hot garnished with parsley.
- **Nutrition Facts:** Per Serving: Calories 237, total Carbs 5g, net Carbs 4g, Fiber 1g, Protein 40g, Fat 5g, saturated Fat 1g, sugar 1g, sodium 589mg, Cholesterol 125mg

119.Super Tasty Tex-mex Chicken

Servings: 2
Cooking Time: 6 Hours
Ingredients:
- 1/2lb of boneless, Skinless Chicken Thighs
- ½ a cup of frozen Onion and Pepper strips, thawed
- ½ a cup of frozen Yellow Corn
- 1/4 of a cup of Water
- ½ a cup of diced Tomatoes and Green Chilies
- ½ a tsp of ground Cumin
- ½ a tsp of Tex-Mex Seasoning

Directions:
1. Sauté the chicken so its browned on both sides and place it in your crockpot
2. Then sauté the onions and peppers until just tender
3. Place the onions and peppers with the chicken and add the water and tomatoes.
4. Cook covered on low for 4 hours and stir in the cumin
5. Cook them for an additional 30 minutes, or until thighs become very tender
6. Serve
- **Nutrition Facts:** Per Serving:Cal 138, total fat 8.3g, sat fat 2g, Chol 48mg, sodium 114mg, Carb 6.4g, fiber 1.2g, protein 10.6g

120.Chicken & Zucchini Stew

Servings: 6
Cooking Time: 4 Hours
Ingredients:
- 2 tbsp. olive oil
- 6 chicken breasts, boneless, skinless & cut in 1-inch pieces
- 8 oz. mushrooms, sliced
- 1 onion, chopped
- 3 cups zucchini, chopped
- 1 cup green bell pepper, chopped
- 4 cloves garlic, diced fine
- 3 tomatoes, chopped
- 6 oz. tomato paste
- ¾ cup water
- 2 tsp thyme
- 2 tsp oregano
- 2 tsp marjoram
- 2 tsp basil

Directions:
1. Heat oil in a large skillet over med-high heat. Add chicken and cook until lightly browned. transfer the chicken to the crock pot.
2. Add the mushrooms, onion, zucchini, and bell pepper to the skillet and cook 3-5 minutes, or until vegetables start to soften.
3. Add the garlic and cook 1 minute more.
4. Add the vegetables to the chicken with the remaining ingredients stir to combine.
5. Add the lid and cook on low heat 4-5 hours or until chicken is cooked through.
- **Nutrition Facts:** Per Serving: Calories 383, total Carbs 13g, net Carbs 10g, Fiber 3g, Protein 57g, Fat 11g, saturated Fat 2g, sugar 7g, sodium 130mg, Cholesterol 172mg

121.Chicken Mushroom Stew

Servings:6
Cooking Time: 5 Hours 45 Minutes
Ingredients:
- 6 chicken breast halves, boneless and skinless
- 8 oz fresh sliced mushroom
- 3 cups zucchini, diced
- 1 cup green pepper, chopped
- 2 tbsp divided canola oil
- 1 diced medium onion
- 4 minced garlic cloves
- 3 chopped medium tomatoes
- 6 oz tomato paste
- ¾ cup water
- 2 tbsp each dried basil
- 2 tbsp thyme
- 2 tbsp marjoram
- 2 tbsp oregano

Directions:
1. Cut the chicken into small cubes and place it in a skillet.
2. Brown the chicken with one tablespoon oil and transfer into a crockpot.
3. Using the same skillet sauté, the mushroom, onion, zucchini, and green pepper in remaining oil until they become tender-crisp then transfer the mixture to the crockpot.
4. Add garlic to the crockpot and cook for one minute.
5. Transfer the mixture into the crockpot and add tomatoes, tomato paste, water, basil, thyme, marjoram, and oregano.
6. cover and cook for five hours
7. Serve and enjoy.
- **Nutrition Facts:** Per Serving:Calories 237, Total Fat 8g, Saturated Fat 1g, Total Carbs 15g, Net Carbs 12g, Protein 27g, Sugar 7g, Fiber 3g, Sodium 82mg

122.Turkey Breast With Gravy

Servings:12
Cooking Time: 6 Hours 15 Minutes
Ingredients:
- 2 tbsp parsley, dried and in flakes
- 1 tbsp poultry seasoning
- 3 medium carrots
- 3 chopped celery ribs
- 6 lb bone-in and skinless turkey breast
- 1tbsp salt
- ½ tbsp paprika
- ½ tbsp pepper
- 2 chopped medium onions
- ½ cup all-purpose flour
- ½ cup water

Directions:
1. Mix parsley, salt, poultry seasoning, paprika and pepper in a bowl
2. Put the onions, carrots, and celery in a crockpot and place the turkey on top.
3. Rub the turkey with the seasoning mixture in the bowl.
4. Cover and cook for six hours.
5. Remove turkey from the crockpot and put it on a chopping board and slice it after fifteen minutes.
6. Put cooking juices into a saucepan.
7. In another bowl, mix flour and water until they become smooth then stir in the mixture into the cooking juices.
8. Heat the mixture as you stir and allow it to boil for two minutes.
9. Serve with the turkey and enjoy it.
- **Nutrition Facts:** Per Serving:Calories 200, Total Fat 1g, Saturated Fat 0g, Total Carbs 2g, Net Carbs 2g, Protein 43g, Sugar 0g, Fiber 0g, Sodium 270mg

123.Chicken Enchiladas

Servings: 6
Cooking Time: 4 Hours
Ingredients:
- 2 chicken breast, boneless
- 1 tsp cumin
- 1 tsp chili powder
- ½ tsp garlic powder
- ½ tsp black pepper
- 4 oz. jalapenos, diced
- 16 oz. jarred enchilada sauce, sugar-free
- 1 cup sour cream, fat-free, divided
- 1 ½ cups cheddar cheese, grated
- 6 medium whole-grain tortillas

Directions:
1. Heat oven to 350 °F.
2. Place chicken in a baking dish and cover. Bake 35-45 minutes or until cooked through.
3. Remove skin from the chicken and shred with 2 forks.
4. In a medium bowl, add chicken and seasonings and mix to coat.
5. stir in jalapenos, ½ cup enchilada sauce, ½ cup sour cream, and 1 cup cheese and mix well.
6. Place ½ cup of mixture in the middle of each tortilla and roll up.
7. Place 3 enchiladas on the bottom of the crock pot and top with some of the sauce. Repeat with remaining enchiladas and sauce.
8. In a small bowl, whisk together remaining enchilada sauce and ½ cup sour cream. Pour over enchiladas. Add lid and cook on low heat 3-4 hours or until bubbly.
9. Carefully remove enchiladas, one at a time, and transfer to a serving plate. top with sauce and sprinkle cheese over. serve immediately.
- **Nutrition Facts:** Per Serving: Calories 294, total Carbs 29g, net Carbs 26g, Fiber 3g, Protein 16g, Fat 13g, saturated Fat 6g, sugar 3g, sodium 422mg, Cholesterol 45mg

124.Greek Chicken Stew

Servings: 8
Cooking Time: 6 Hours
Ingredients:
- 3 tbsp. extra virgin olive oil
- 8 chicken thighs, boneless
- 1 tsp salt
- 1 tsp pepper
- 1 tbsp. Greek seasoning
- 1 cup onion, chopped
- 2 tbsp. fresh lemon juice
- 2 tsp fresh oregano, chopped
- 4 cloves garlic, peeled
- 2 tbsp. garlic, diced fine
- 1 cup chicken broth, low sodium
- 1 cup Kalamata olives, pitted
- ½ cup roasted red pepper, chopped
- 1 tbsp. capers, drained
- ¼ cup sundried tomatoes, chopped
- 4 cups cauliflower, grated

Directions:
1. Heat oil in a large skillet over med-high heat.
2. sprinkle chicken with salt, pepper, and Greek seasoning.
3. Cook in the skillet until brown on both sides. transfer to the crock pot.
4. Add onion, lemon juice, and oregano to the skillet and cook until onion begins to soften.
5. Add garlic and cook 1 minute more. Add to chicken.
6. Add the remaining ingredients and stir to mix.
7. Add the lid and cook on low heat 5-6 hours, or until chicken is cooked through.
- **Nutrition Facts:** Per Serving: Calories 470, total Carbs 8g, net Carbs 5g, Fiber 3g, Protein 52g, Fat 25g, saturated Fat 5g, sugar 3g, sodium 619mg, Cholesterol 49mg

125.Turkey In Cream Sauce

Servings:8
Cooking Time: 8 Hours 15 Minutes
Ingredients:
- 1 ¼ cups white wine
- 2 bay leaves
- 2 tbsp crushed and dried rosemary
- ¾ lb turkey breast tenderloins each
- ½ cup whole or cream
- 1 chopped medium onion
- 2 minced garlic cloves
- ½ tbsp pepper
- 3 tbsp cornstarch
- ½ tbsp salt

Directions:
1. Add wine, onion, garlic, and bay leaves in a crockpot.
2. Mix rosemary and pepper in a bowl, then rub over the turkey and put them in the crockpot.
3. Cover the crockpot and cook for eight hours.
4. When time is done, remove the turkey and put it in a serving platter
5. Skim fat from cooking juice, put the juice in a saucepan and heat to boil.
6. In the hot liquid stir in cornstarch, cream, and salt and allow it boil it for two minutes.
7. Serve with turkey and enjoy it.
- **Nutrition Facts:** Per Serving:Calories 205, Total Fat 3g, Saturated Fat 1g, Total Carbs 6g, Net Carbs 5g, Protein 32g, Sugar 1g, Fiber 0g, Sodium 231mg

126.Polynesian Chicken

Servings: 6
Cooking Time: 6 Hours
Ingredients:
- 20 oz. pineapple chunks, in natural juice
- 1 tbsp. soy sauce, low sodium
- 1 clove garlic, diced fine
- 1 tsp fresh ginger, grated
- 1/3 cup honey
- 1 tbsp. cornstarch
- 4 chicken breasts, boneless, skinless, cut in 1-inch pieces
- 8 oz. can water chestnuts, drain & slice
- 1 red bell pepper, cut in 1-inch strips

Directions:
1. In a small bowl, whisk together juice from the pineapple, soy sauce, garlic, ginger, and honey until combined.
2. Add cornstarch and mix well.
3. Place chicken in the crock pot and pour the sauce over. Add the lid and cook on low heat 4-6 hours, or until chicken is cooked through.
4. Add the bell pepper, chestnuts, and pineapple during the last 30 minutes of cooking time. serve immediately.
- **Nutrition Facts:** Per Serving: Calories 255, total Carbs 31g, net Carbs 29g, Fiber 2g, Protein 18g, Fat 7g, saturated Fat 2g, sugar 16g, sodium 468mg, Cholesterol 24mg

127.Caribbean Curried Chicken

Servings:8
Cooking Time: 6 Hours 15 Minutes
Ingredients:
- 1 tbsp madras curry powder
- 4 0z chicken thigh boneless and skinless
- 1 sliced medium onion
- 1 ½ cups Goya mojo Criollo marinade
- 1 tbsp garlic powder
- 1 tbsp pepper
- 1 tbsp canola oil
- 2 tbsp all-purpose flour
- Green onions for serving
- Cilantro leaves for serving

Directions:
1. Mix madras curry powder, garlic powder, and pepper in a bowl and sprinkle it over chicken as you press so that it can adhere properly.
2. Put the chicken in a crockpot and sprinkle onions on it.
3. Pour mojo criollo marinade on the sides of the crockpot avoiding contact with the chicken.
4. Cover and cook for six hours.
5. Remove the chicken from heat and put it in a hot dish.
6. Put cooking juice from the crockpot in a cup and skim fat.
7. In a saucepan, pour oil and heat it as you whisk in flour until smooth.
8. Pour the cooking juices into the mixture.
9. Stir cook the mixture and allow it to boil for two minutes so that the mixture thickens.
10. Add the chicken into the mixture and simmer for five minutes.
11. Serve with rice, green onions, and cilantro and enjoy.
- **Nutrition Facts:** Per Serving:Calories 249, Total Fat 13g, Saturated Fat 3g, Total Carbs 11g, Net Carbs 10g, Protein 22g, Sugar 5g, Fiber 1g, Sodium 514mg

128.Curried Chicken & Peppers

Servings: 6
Cooking Time: 2 ½ Hours
Ingredients:
- 1 red bell pepper, cut in 1/2-inch strips
- 1 yellow bell pepper, cut in 1/2-inch strips
- 1 onion, cut in thin wedges
- ¼ cup golden raisins
- 3 cloves garlic, diced fine
- 3 lbs.chicken thighs, boneless & skinless
- 14 ½ oz. diced tomatoes, undrained
- 2 tsp curry powder
- 1 tsp cumin
- 2 tbsp. flour

Directions:
1. Place the peppers, onion, raisins, garlic, and chicken in the crock pot.
2. In a mixing bowl, combine tomatoes, seasonings, and flour until mixed well. Pour over chicken.
3. Add the lid and cook on high 2 ½ - 3 hours, or on low 5-6 hours until chicken is cooked through and tender.
- **Nutrition Facts:** Per Serving: Calories 521, total Carbs 17g, net Carbs 15g, Fiber 2g, Protein 65g, Fat21 g, saturated Fat 5g, sugar 7g, sodium 1446mg, Cholesterol 293mg

129.Tender Chicken With Zucchini Noodles And Basil Pesto

Servings: 2
Cooking Time: 8 Hours
Ingredients:
- 6oz of Chicken Breasts, sliced
- 2 cups of hand sliced or spiralized Zucchini Noodles
- 1 cup of fresh sliced Mushrooms
- 1 small chopped Red Onion
- 2 cloves of finely chopped Garlic
- 4 fresh, finely chopped Basil Leaves
- 1 tbsp of Basil Pesto Sauce
- 1 tsp Olive Oil

Directions:
1. Sauté the onion in your crockpot or a pan until translucent, then add the garlic and cook until fragrant
2. Then add the mushrooms, chicken, pesto and zucchini noodles stirring to combine
3. If you used a saucepan to sauté, place the mixture in your slow cooker or if you sautéed in your slow cooker, just cover it and cook on the lowest setting, for 8 hours or high for 4 hours
4. Then serve
- **Nutrition Facts:** Per Serving:246 cal, 9g total fat, 2g sat fat, 72mg chol, 172mg sodium, 12g carb, 3g fiber, 31g protein

130.Lovely Chicken With Oranges, And Yellow Capsicum

Servings: 2
Cooking Time: 7 Hours
Ingredients:
- 4 Chicken Drum Sticks
- 1 Orange, peeled and sliced into rings
- 1 small Yellow sliced Capsicum
- ½ a cup of Tomato Salsa or crushed Tomatoes with Basil
- ½ a cup of Chicken Stock
- 1 small, Medium, Hot Chili, deseeded and sliced
- 1 small, thinly sliced Onion
- 1 clove of minced Garlic
- 1 cup of Quinoa
- Sea Salt and Black Pepper to taste
- ¼ a cup of chopped fresh Cilantro Leaves

Directions:
1. Place the quinoa in your crockpot with the chicken drumsticks
2. Pour the stock and salsa over the chicken
3. Add the capsicum, garlic, chili and onion
4. Place the orange rings on top of the chicken
5. Cook covered on low for 7 hours
6. Serve with the fresh cilantro leaves
- **Nutrition Facts:** Per Serving:Cal 734, total fat 25.6g, sat fat 6.7g, chol 180mg, sodium 354mg, carb 76.7g fiber 10.8g, protein 53.5g

131.Chicken Noodle Soup

Servings:6
Cooking Time: 5 Hours
Ingredients:
- 12 baby carrots, fresh
- 4 celery ribs
- 1 tbsp parsley, minced
- 1 ¼ lb chicken breast halves and thighs each, boneless and skinless
- 14 ½ oz chicken broth
- ¾ cup onions, finely chopped
- ½ tbsp pepper
- ¼ tbsp cayenne pepper
- 1tbsp mustard seed
- 2 peeled and halved garlic cloves
- 9 oz refrigerated linguine
- Pepper to taste, coarsely ground

Directions:
1. Add carrots, celery ribs, onion, parsley, pepper, and cayenne pepper in a crockpot.
2. Put mustard seed and garlic in a spice bag with a double thickness and add to the crockpot.
3. Add chicken breast, thigh, and broth to the pot, cover, and set the timer for six hours.
4. When time elapses, remove the chicken from the crockpot and place it on a chopping board. Discard the spice bag.
5. Stir in the linguine, cover, and cook for thirty minutes.
6. Cut the chicken into pieces and add it to the soup. Heat through and sprinkle ground pepper into the soup.
7. Serve and enjoy.
- **Nutrition Facts:** Per Serving:Calories 199, Total Fat 6g, Saturated Fat 2g, Total Carbs 14g, Net Carbs 11g, Protein 22g, Sugar 2g, Fiber 1g, Sodium 663mg

132.Moroccan Chicken With Apricots, Olives And Almonds

Servings: 2
Cooking Time: 4 Hours
Ingredients:
- 1lbs of skinless Chicken Thighs
- 1 small Onion, cut into 1/2-inch wedges
- 1 tsp of Ground Cumin
- 1/2 a tsp of Ground Ginger
- 1/2 a tsp of Ground Coriander
- ¼ of a tsp of Ground Cinnamon
- 1/4 of a tsp of Cayenne Pepper
- 1 Bay Leaf
- 1/3 of a cup of low-sodium Chicken Stock or Broth
- ½ a cup of drained and rinsed Chickpeas
- 1/2 a cup of Green Olives
- ¼ of a cup of dried Apricots
- ¼ of a cup of Sliced Almonds
- Sea Salt and ground Black Pepper to taste

Directions:
1. Place the chicken with the onion, cumin, ginger, coriander, cinnamon and cayenne in a bowl and season with salt and pepper before mixing well
2. Place the chicken and onion mixture in your crockpot
3. Add the bay leaf and cook, covered, on high for 2 hours
4. Stir in the chickpeas, olives, and apricots, then cook for another two hours or until the apricots have become plump and the chicken is tender
5. Adjust the seasoning if necessary and remove the bay leaf
6. Toast the almonds until they are golden and fragrant
7. Place the chicken and accompanying juices in 2 bowls, sprinkle them with almonds and serve with Couscous
- **Nutrition Facts:** Per Serving:866 cal, 30g total fat, 7.4g sat fat, 389mg sodium, 34.8g carb, 10g fiber, 109.4g protein

133.Turkey Sausage & Barley Soup

Servings: 6
Cooking Time: 5 Hours
Ingredients:
- 1 lb. turkey sausage
- 1 onion, chopped
- 1 cup carrot, peel & dice
- ½ cup pearl barley
- 3 ½ cups chicken broth, low sodium
- 1 tsp salt
- ½ tsp black pepper
- 2 (15 oz) cans petite diced tomatoes
- 1 tbsp. tomato paste
- 3 cups kale, chopped

Directions:
1. Heat a skillet over medium heat. Add the sausage and cook, breaking up with a spatula, until no longer pink. drain off fat and transfer sausage to the crock pot.
2. Add onion, carrot, barley, broth, salt, pepper, and tomatoes. stir to mix.
3. Add the lid and cook on low heat 4 – 4/12 hours or until barley is tender.
4. stir in the tomato paste and kale. Cover and cook another 30 minutes until the kale has wilted. serve immediately.
- **Nutrition Facts:** Per Serving: Calories 279 total Carbs 29g, net Carbs 21g, Fiber 8g, Protein 23g, Fat 9g, saturated Fat 2g, sugar 9g, sodium 704mg, Cholesterol 61mg

134.Heavenly Spicy Chicken With Quinoa

Servings: 2
Cooking Time: 7 Hours
Ingredients:
- 1/2lb of Chicken Breasts or Boneless Chicken Thighs
- 1 cup of cooked Quinoa
- 1 tbsp of Tamari sauce or Coconut Aminos
- 1 tbsp of Raw Honey
- 2 tbsp of a cup of Rice Wine Vinegar or Apple Cider Vinegar
- 1 tbsp of Mirin or dry Sherry)
- 1 tsp of Toasted Sesame Oil
- 1 clove of minced Garlic
- 1 tsp of minced Ginger
- ¼ of a tsp of Red Chili Flakes (optional)
- Sea Salt and freshly ground Black Pepper, to taste
- 1 tbsp of Corn Starch
- 1 tbsp of fresh Water
- For garnish: sliced green onions, sesame seeds

Directions:
1. Season the chicken well with salt and pepper, then sauté it in your crockpot or a hot pan to seal
2. Whisk the mirin, tamari sauce, vinegar, honey, sesame oil, ginger and garlic, then pour this over the chicken in your crockpot
3. Cook it covered on low for 6 to 7 hours or high for 3 to 4 hours
4. When the chicken is tender, add the cornstarch mixed with the water stirring until thicken
5. Serve on top of the quinoa
- **Nutrition Facts:** Per Serving:65 cal, total fat 6g, sat fat 2 g, 53g carb, 124 chol, 1271mg, sodium, , 1g fiber, 44g protein

135.Parmesan Herb Chicken & Orzo

Servings: 2
Cooking Time: 4 Hours
Ingredients:
- 1 boneless and skinless Chicken Breasts
- 1 cup of low sodium Chicken Stock
- 1 cup of Orzo Pasta
- 1 tbsp of Unsalted Butter, melted
- 1 cup of sliced Mushrooms
- 1 small finely chopped Onion
- 1 clove of minced Garlic
- Sea Salt (or to taste)
- ¼ of a tsp of freshly ground Black Pepper
- ¼ of a cup of shaved Parmesan Cheese
- Freshly cracked black pepper and herbs (such as thyme or parsley) for garnish
- 3 teaspoons Italian seasoning, divided

Directions:
1. Season the chicken well with Italian seasonings and salt and pepper
2. Seal and brown the chicken in your crockpot or a large pan
3. Add half a cup of the stock, the mushrooms, butter, garlic, onions, salt and pepper
4. Cook the chicken covered on high for 1-2 hours or on low for 3-4 hours
5. Cook the orzo in half a cup of stock
6. Once the chicken is tender, take it from the crockpot and place the cooked orzo in the mixture left, the stir to incorporate it
7. Return the chicken to your crockpot and place it on top of the orzo mixture
8. Sprinkle the Parmesan cheese on top of the chicken, replace the lid and cook, covered a for 15 minutes
9. Serve with fresh herbs and cracked black pepper
- **Nutrition Facts:** Per Serving:417 cal, 16.5g sat fat, 124mg chol, 22g carb, 462mg sodium, 0.8g fiber, 17g protein

136.Italian Chicken With Sweet Potatoes

Servings: 4
Cooking Time: 6 Hours
Ingredients:
- 4 chicken breasts, boneless & skinless
- 8 oz. cremini mushrooms, halved
- 2 cups sweet potatoes, chopped
- ¼ cup fresh lemon juice
- ½ cup chicken broth, low sodium
- ¼ cup extra-virgin olive oil
- 1 tsp oregano
- 1 tsp parsley
- 1 tsp basil
- 1 tsp salt
- ½ tsp black pepper
- ½ tsp onion powder
- 2 cloves garlic, diced fine

Directions:
1. Place the chicken in the middle of the crock pot.
2. Place potatoes on one side, and mushrooms on the other side of the chicken.
3. In a medium bowl, whisk together the remaining ingredients and pour over chicken and vegetables.
4. Add the lid and cook on low heat 4-6 hours, or on high 3-4 hours until chicken is cooked through and potatoes are tender.
- **Nutrition Facts:** Per Serving: Calories 364, total Carbs 33g, net Carbs 28g, Fiber 5g, Protein 24g, Fat 16g, saturated Fat 2g, sugar 8g, sodium 700mg, Cholesterol 62mg

137.Delicious Chicken, Corn And Bean Chili

Servings:2
Cooking Time: 6 Hours
Ingredients:
- ½lb of cubed Chicken breasts
- ½ a cup of chopped Onion
- 1 tbsp of Coconut or Olive Oil
- ¼ of a cup of rinsed Cannellini Beans
- 1/2 a cup of Diced Tomatoes liquid included
- 1 tbsp of mild Green Chilies
- ¼ of a cup of Frozen Yellow Corn
- 1 tsp of minced Garlic
- ¼ of a tsp of Ground Cumin
- ¼ tsp celery salt
- ¼ tsp of Ground Coriander
- Sea Salt and Black Pepper to taste
- Sour Cream and Shredded Cheddar for serving

Directions:
1. Sauté the chicken and onions in your crockpot or a fry pan
2. Add the beans, corn, tomatoes and spices
3. Cook covered on low for 5 hours or until the chicken is tender
4. Serve with sour cream and cheese
- **Nutrition Facts:** Per Serving:Cal 304, Fat 10g, Sat fat 1g, Carbs 22g, Protein 30g, Fiber 5g, Chol 75mg, Sodium 455mg, Calcium 66mg

138.Teriyaki Chicken & "rice"

Servings: 6
Cooking Time: 4 Hours
Ingredients:
- 2 tbsp. cornstarch
- ½ cup + 2 tbsp. water
- ¾ cup soy sauce, low sodium
- ¼ cup stevia brown sugar
- ½ tsp ginger
- ½ tsp garlic, diced fine
- 12 oz. bag stir fry vegetables
- 3 cups cauliflower, grated
- 2 chicken breasts, boneless & skinless

Directions:
1. In a measuring cup, stir together cornstarch and 2 tablespoons water until smooth.
2. In a small saucepan, combine soy sauce, ½ cup water, stevia, ginger, and garlic. Cover and bring to a boil over medium heat.
3. Remove lid and stir in cornstarch mixture. Cook until the sauce starts to thicken, about 1 minute.
4. spray the crock pot with cooking spray. Place the vegetables on the bottom of the crock pot.
5. Lay the chicken on top of the vegetables and pour the sauce over the top.
6. Add the lid and cook on low heat 4 hours, or until chicken is tender.
7. Remove the chicken and using 2 forks shred it. Return the chicken back to the crock pot and stir everything together. serve.
- **Nutrition Facts:** Per Serving: Calories 143, total Carbs 18g, net Carbs 16g, Fiber 2g, Protein 22g, Fat 2g, saturated Fat 0g, sugar 2g, sodium 1208mg, Cholesterol 57mg

139.Chicken Satay

Servings: 4
Cooking Time: 4 Hours
Ingredients:
- 1 tbsp. olive oil
- 6 chicken tenders, boneless & skinless
- 1 stalk lemongrass, chopped
- 1/3 cup coconut milk, unsweetened
- 2 tbsp. fish sauce
- 1 tbsp. fresh lime juice
- 1 tbsp. lite soy sauce
- 1 tsp sriracha sauce
- 1 tsp stevia
- 1 tsp ginger
- 1 tsp turmeric
- 2 cloves garlic, diced fine

Directions:
1. Heat oil in a large skillet over med-high heat.
2. Add chicken and cook until browned on the outside. transfer to the crock pot.
3. In a medium bowl, stir together remaining ingredients and pour over chicken.
4. Add the lid and cook on low heat 3-4 hours, or on high 2-3 hours until chicken is cooked through.
- **Nutrition Facts:** Per Serving: Calories 375, total Carbs 8g, net Carbs 7g, Fiber 1g, Protein 25g, Fat 25g, saturated Fat 10g, sugar 4g, sodium 927mg, Cholesterol 96mg

140.Alluring Turkey With Mushroom Sauce

Servings: 2
Cooking Time: 7 Hours
Ingredients:
- 1 small (1lb) turkey breast
- 1 tbsp of Unsalted Butter
- 1 tbsp of Dried Parsley Flakes
- ½ a tsp of Dried Tarragon Flakes
- ½ a tsp of Sea Salt
- ¼ of a tsp of Freshly Ground Black Pepper
- ¼ of a cup of Chicken Broth
- ¼ of a cup of Dry White Wine
- 1 cup of finely sliced Fresh Mushrooms
- 1 tbsp of Cornstarch

Directions:
1. Place the turkey in your crockpot and brush it with the butter
2. Sprinkle the mushrooms, tarragon, parsley, salt and pepper over it and pour the wine and stock around it
3. Cook covered on low for 8 hours
4. Remove the turkey and slice it into 2 portions.
5. Skim off any excess fat and turn the crockpot to high setting
6. Combine the cornstarch with a little water and add it to the juices and mushrooms in the crockpot, stirring constantly until thickened then serve over or beside the turkey
- **Nutrition Facts:** Per Serving:Cal 308, Fat 14g Sat fat 5g, carbs 3g, Protein 38g, Chol 118mg, Sodium 327mg, Calcium 31mg

141.Chicken Cacciatore

Servings: 6
Cooking Time: 4 Hours
Ingredients:
- 1/3 cup flour
- 3-4 lbs. chicken, skinless & cut in pieces
- 2 tbsp. olive oil
- 2 onions, cut in wedges
- 1 green bell pepper, cut in strips
- 6 oz. mushrooms, sliced
- 14 oz. tomatoes, diced, undrained
- 2 cloves garlic, diced fine
- 1/8 tsp salt
- ½ tsp oregano
- ¼ tsp basil
- ½ cup Parmesan cheese, grated

Directions:
1. Place flour in a large plastic bag. Add chicken, a few pieces at a time, and shake to coat.
2. Heat oil in a large skillet over medium heat. Add chicken and brown on both sides. transfer chicken to the crock pot.
3. Place the onions, bell pepper, and mushrooms over the chicken.
4. In a small bowl, combine tomatoes, garlic, and seasonings. Pour over the vegetables.
5. Add the lid and cook on low heat 4-5 hours or until chicken is cooked through and vegetables are tender.
6. transfer to a serving plate and garnish with parmesan cheese before serving.
- **Nutrition Facts:** Per Serving: Calories 474, total Carbs 15g, net Carbs 13g, Fiber 2g, Protein 67g, Fat 15g, saturated Fat 4g, sugar 4g, sodium 436mg, Cholesterol 204mg

142.Tomato Balsamic Crockpot Chicken

Servings:6
Cooking Time: 7 Hours
Ingredients:
- 2 chopped medium carrots
- 2lb chicken thighs, bone-in and skinless
- ½ cup chicken broth, reduced-sodium
- 1 bay leaf
- Orzo, hot cooked
- ½ cup shallot, sliced
- 1tbsp flour, all-purpose
- 14½ oz tomatoes, diced and undrained
- ¼ cup vinegar, balsamic
- 1tbsp olive oil
- 2 minced garlic cloves
- ½ tbsp Italian seasoning
- ½ tbsp salt
- ¼ tbsp pepper

Directions:
1. Put carrots and shallots in a crockpot and place the chicken on top.
2. Whisk flour and broth in a bowl until smooth, then stir in tomatoes, vinegar, oil, garlic, bay leaf, and seasoning.
3. Pour the mixture in the bowl over the chicken, cover, and cook for seven hours.
4. When time is done, remove the chicken and place it on a chopping board and discard bay leaf
5. Remove the bones from chicken bones and return it to the crockpot then heat through.
6. Serve with orzo and enjoy
- **Nutrition Facts:** Per Serving:Calories 235, Total Fat 11g, Saturated Fat 3g, Total Carbs 12g, Net Carbs 10g, Protein 23g, Sugar 7g, Fiber 2g, Sodium 433mg

143.Lovely Roasted Red Capsicum Chicken

Servings: 2
Cooking Time: 4 Hours
Ingredients:
- 2 medium Chicken Breasts
- 1 medium diced Onion
- 2 cloves of minced Garlic
- ½ a cup of roughly chopped Roasted, Red Capsicum
- ½ a cup of Kalamata Olives
- 1 tbsp of Capers
- 1 tbsp of fresh Lemon Juice
- 2 tsp of Italian Seasoning
- Sea Salt and freshly ground Black Pepper to taste
- Olive Oil as Needed
- Fresh herbs like Basil or Thyme to Garnish

Directions:
1. Use salt and pepper to season the chicken before sauté it for 2 minutes on each side
2. Transfer the chicken to your well-oiled crockpot
3. Add the red peppers, onions, olives and capers to your slow cooker around and on the sides of the chicken
4. Mix together the Italian seasoning, lemon juice and garlic and spread this over the chicken
5. Cook covered on low for 4 hours or on high for 2 hours. Garnish with fresh thyme or oregano, then serve hot
- **Nutrition Facts:** Per Serving:cal 325, total fat.13g, sat fat 13g, chol 128mg, sodium 113mg, carb 8.5g, fiber 1.8g, protein 41.7g

144.Balsamic Chicken

Servings: 10
Cooking Time: 4 Hours
Ingredients:
- 1 tbsp. olive oil
- 6 chicken breasts, boneless & skinless
- salt & pepper, to taste
- 1 onion, sliced thin
- 1 tsp oregano
- 1 tsp basil
- 1 tsp rosemary
- ½ tsp thyme
- 4 cloves garlic
- ½ cup balsamic vinegar
- 2 (14 ½ oz) can tomatoes, diced

Directions:
1. Pour the oil in the crock pot and add the chicken.
2. sprinkle salt and pepper over each piece of chicken.
3. top chicken with onion, herbs, and garlic.
4. Pour vinegar over the top then add tomatoes, undrained.
5. Add the lid and cook on high 4 hours, or until chicken is cooked through.
6. Remove chicken and slice, serve over pasta topped with sauce.
- **Nutrition Facts:** Per Serving: Calories 238, total Carbs 7g, net Carbs 5g, Fiber 2g, Protein 25g, Fat 12g, saturated Fat 3g, sugar 4g, sodium 170mg, Cholesterol 73mg

145.Southern Fried Chicken

Servings: 2
Cooking Time: 2 ½ Hours
Ingredients:
- nonstick cooking spray
- 2 chicken breast, boneless & skinless
- ½ cup buttermilk, reduced fat
- ½ cup white whole wheat flour
- ¼ tsp black pepper
- ¼ tsp smoked paprika
- ¼ tsp garlic powder
- ¼ tsp salt
- ½ cup whole-wheat panko bread crumbs

Directions:
1. spray the crock pot with cooking spray.
2. Add the buttermilk to a small bowl.
3. In a separate bowl, combine flour and seasonings.
4. Place the bread crumbs in a shallow dish.
5. dip each chicken in the buttermilk, dredge in flour mixture, then dip in buttermilk again.
6. Press the chicken into the bread crumbs to thoroughly coat both sides. Place in the crock pot.
7. Add the lid and cook on high 2 ½ hours or until chicken is cooked through. Remove the lid and cook another 10 minutes to crisp the chicken. serve.
- **Nutrition Facts:** Per Serving: Calories 379, total Carbs 36g, net Carbs 32g, Fiber 4g, Protein 31g, Fat 12g, saturated Fat 3g, sugar 4g, sodium 446mg, Cholesterol 73mg

146.Chicken & Wild Rice Soup

Servings: 8
Cooking Time: 6 Hours
Ingredients:

- 1 cup wild rice, uncooked
- 3 chicken breasts, boneless & skinless
- 1 cup onion, diced small
- ½ cup carrot, peeled & diced small
- ½ cup celery, peeled & diced small
- 6 cups chicken broth, low sodium
- ½ tsp sage
- ¼ tsp thyme
- ¼ tsp rosemary
- ½ tsp salt
- ½ tsp black pepper
- 2 cups plain Greek yogurt
- ¼ cup fresh parsley, chopped

Directions:

1. Rinse the rice and place it in the crock pot.
2. Add chicken, vegetables, broth, and seasonings, stir to mix.
3. Add the lid and cook on high 3-4 hours, or on low 6-8 hours, until chicken is cooked through and tender.
4. Remove chicken to a bowl and shred. Return it to the crock pot along with the yogurt. stir until smooth. (If you like a thicker consistency, mix equal parts cornstarch and water and stir into soup. Cook until soup reaches desired consistency). serve garnished with parsley.
- **Nutrition Facts:** Per Serving: Calories 250, total Carbs 22g, net Carbs 20g, Fiber 2g, Protein 26g, Fat 7g, saturated Fat 3g, sugar 4g, sodium 246mg, Cholesterol 56mg

147.Cheesy Chicken Broccoli Casserole

Servings: 2
Cooking Time: 4 Hours
Ingredients:

- 1/2lb of Chicken Breast, chopped into 1 inch pieces
- ½ a cup of Raw Broccoli Florets
- 1 cup uncooked Brown Rice
- 1/2 of a diced Red Onion
- 1 tbsp of minced Garlic
- 1 tsp of Thyme
- 1 tsp of Rosemary
- 2 cups of Chicken Stock or Broth
- ½ a cup of Greek Yogurt
- 2/3 of a cup of mixed cheeses such as Monterey Jack, Parmesan, Cheddar
- 1 tbsp of Olive Oil
- Sea Salt and freshly ground Black Pepper to taste

Directions:

1. Sauté the garlic and onion for a few minutes in the olive oil
2. Add the uncooked rice, the fresh rosemary and fresh thyme
3. Then add the diced chicken and stock
4. Cook covered on high for 3 to 5 hours
5. About an hour before serving the chicken, add the yogurt and cheeses, stirring well to combine completely
6. Place the raw broccoli florets straight on top of the rice without stirring them in, allowing them to cook in the steam and remain crunchy
- **Nutrition Facts:** Per Serving:790 cal, fat 27.2g, sat fat 10.4g chol 116mg, sodium 1093mg, 52.1g protein, 82.2g carb, 5g fiber

148.Slow Simmered Crockpot Chicken With Raisins, Capers And Basil

Servings:8
Cooking Time: 5 Hours
Ingredients:
- 4oz chicken thigh, boneless, skinless, and cut into 8 pieces
- 8 oz mushrooms, sliced
- ½ cup golden raisins
- ¼ cup basil, chopped
- Hot cooked couscous
- 2 tbsp divided olive oil
- 1tbsp salt
- 1 tbsp pepper
- ½ cup marsala wine
- 1sliced medium sweet red pepper
- 1 sliced medium onion
- 14 ½ tomatoes, diced

Directions:
1. Heat one tablespoon oil in a skillet.
2. Spread the chicken on a chopping board and sprinkle it with salt and pepper.
3. Brown the chicken with oil and transfer it to a crockpot.
4. Stir in the wine in the skillet to loosen the bits and add it to the crockpot.
5. Stir in mushrooms, red pepper, onion, and tomatoes to the crockpot.
6. Cover the crockpot and cook for five hours.
7. Sprinkle the delicacy with basil.
8. Serve with couscous and enjoy.
- **Nutrition Facts:** Per Serving:Calories 250, Total Fat 12g, Saturated Fat 3g, Total Carbs 13g, Net Carbs 11g, Protein 23g, Sugar 9g, Fiber 2g, Sodium 494mg

149.Chicken And Mushroom Supreme

Servings:2
Cooking Time: 4 Hours
Ingredients:
- ½ a cup of Whole Grain Flour
- 1lb of Broiler Chicken into bite sized pieces
- 1 tsp of Coconut or Olive Oil
- 1 medium Onion, sliced into wedges
- 1 small sliced Capsicum
- 1 cup of finely sliced Fresh Mushrooms
- 1 clove of minced Garlic
- ½ a cup of Diced Tomatoes
- ½ a cup of Chicken Stock
- ½ a tsp of Dried Oregano
- ½ a tsp of Dried Basil
- Sea Salt and Black Pepper to taste
- ¼ of a cup of Shredded Parmesan Cheese

Directions:
1. Place the flour and ¼ of a tsp of salt and pepper in a plastic bag, then add a few pieces of the chicken at a time and shake to coat them evenly
2. Sauté the chicken in your crockpot or a heavy pan to brown. Then place them in your crockpot
3. Add the onions, capsicum, mushrooms, tomatoes, garlic, chicken stock, oregano and basil and cook covered for 5 hours or the chicken and vegetables are tender
4. Serve the chicken garnished with Parmesan cheese
- **Nutrition Facts:** Per Serving:Cal 277, Fat 11g, Sat fat 3g, Carbs 15g, protein 29g, fiber 2g, Chol 85mg, Sodium 463mg, Calcium 146mg

150.Tender Crockpot Duck

Servings: 2
Cooking Time:7 Hours

Ingredients:
- 1 whole Duck
- 2 medium whole Carrots
- 1 medium Onion
- 2 sticks of Celery
- 4 small whole potatoes
- 2 sprigs of fresh Rosemary
- 1 small bunch of fresh Thyme
- 1 medium whole Orange
- 1 large piece of Cheesecloth (to help lift the duck from your crockpot)

Directions:
1. Remove the duck giblets and remove any visible fat, then wash it in clean fresh water
2. Dry the duck and rub it inside and out with salt and pepper
3. Quarter the onion and orange and place them inside the duck with the sprigs of thyme and rosemary
4. Use the sauté option or a fry pan to brown the outside of the duck
5. Place the vegetables in such a way as to make a stand at the bottom of your crockpot to keep the duck above the liquid
6. Place the duck on the cheesecloth and prick the skin several times to allow any fat to escape, then tie the cheesecloth to encase the bird and make a handle to lift it out when cooked
7. Cook covered on low for 7 hours or high for 4 hours. About half way through cooking, check that the fat (liquid) level is below the duck, if not remove it using a syringe or spoon
8. When cooked, remove the duck from your crockpot, remove the cheese cloth and allow it to sit for 10 minutes before slicing
- **Nutrition Facts:** Per Serving:Cal 281, total fat 14.1g, sat fat 4.7g, chol 27mg, sodium 38mg, carb31.9g, fiber 7.4g, protein 7.2g

SOUPS & STEWS

151.Rutabaga Stew

Servings:15
Cooking Time: 4 Hours 5minutes
Ingredients:

- 24-ounce chicken, diced
- 4 rutabagas, peeled and diced
- 4 beets peeled and diced
- 4 carrots, diced
- 3 stalks celery, diced
- Cooking oil
- 1 red onion diced

Directions:

1. Heat cooking oil in a crockpot.
2. Stir cook chicken in hot oil until brown, about five minutes.
3. Add beets, rutabagas, carrots, onions, and celery to the pot,
4. Add enough water to cover completely.
5. Turn to low and simmer for at least 4 hours, add water to keep vegetables submerged.
6. Serve and enjoy
- **Nutrition Facts:** Per Serving:Calories 111, total fats 2.1g, saturated fat 0.0g, total carbs 12.9g, net carbs 9.0, protein10.7g, sugar 8g, fiber 3.9g, sodium 80mg, potassium 560mg.

152.Dreamy Mediterranean Fish Soup

Servings:2
Cooking Time: 4.5 Hours
Ingredients:

- ¼lb of Cod fillets, cubed
- ¼lb of Shrimp
- 1 small diced Onion
- 1 small Green diced Capsicum
- 2 cloves of minced Garlic
- ½ of a cup of Diced Tomatoes
- 1 cup of Chicken Stock or Broth
- ¼ of a cup of Tomato Sauce
- ¼ of a cup of canned Mushrooms
- 1 tbsp of a cup of sliced Black Olives
- ¼ of a cup of fresh Orange Juice
- ¼ of a cup of Dry White Wine (nice drinking wine)
- 1 Bay Leaf
- 1 tsp of Dried Basil
- 1/8 of a tsp of Fennel Seed, crushed
- 1/8 of a tsp of Freshly Cracked Black Pepper

Directions:

1. Place everything except the fish and shrimp in your crockpot and cook for about 4 to 4.1/2 hours
2. Add the fresh fish 45 minutes before serving and the fresh shrimp 15 minutes before serving
3. Remove the bay leaf and serve
- **Nutrition Facts:** Per Serving:207cal, 3.1g total fat, 0.6 sat fat, 128.1mg chol, 1200.2mg sodium, 12.2 carb, 2.5g fiber, 28.9g protein

153.Coconut Shrimp Curry Recipe

Servings:6
Cooking Time: 2 Hours
Ingredients:
- 1 lb cooked shrimp
- 1 cup chicken broth
- 1 tbsp ground ginger
- 1 bunch lemongrass
- 1 tbsp cilantro
- 14 oz coconut milk
- ¼ Cup lemon juice

Directions:
1. Add all your ingredients in your crockpot.
2. Cook on high for two hours.
3. Eat as it is, or serve with spaghetti squash.
- **Nutrition Facts:** Per Serving:Calories 293, total fats 17.9g, saturated fats 14.9, total carbs 15.1g, net carbs13.5g, protein 20.4g, sugar 2.6g, fiber 1.6g, sodium 326mg, potassium 631mg.

154.Divine Lebanese Red Lentil Soup

Servings:2
Cooking Time: 5 Hours
Ingredients:
- 1 cup of Dry Red Lentils
- 2 cups of Vegetable Stock or Broth
- 1 small chopped Yellow Onion
- 1 small chopped Red Onion
- 1 chopped Carrot
- 1 chopped stalk of Celery leaves included
- 4 cloves of minced Garlic
- 1 tsp of Red Wine Vinegar
- 1 tbsp of Olive Oil
- 1 tsp of Ground Black Cumin
- 1 tsp of Paprika
- Cayenne Pepper to taste
- 1 Bay Leaf
- Fresh chopped Cilantro Leaves for garnish
- A Lemon or Lime sliced into wedges

Directions:
1. Sauté the yellow onion with the carrots and celery in the oil for a few minutes
2. Add the garlic, paprika, cumin, and cayenne, then continue cooking until fragrant about 2 minutes
3. Pour the mixture into your crockpot and add the red lentils, stock, bay leaves and a little salt. Stir and cover
4. Cook covered on low for 4 to 5 hours
5. Check the flavor and add more stock and salt if needed
6. Once the lentils and vegetables have become tender, remove the bay leaf and blend in your blender until smooth. Taste and adjust the seasoning if needed
7. Serve in bowls with the red onion, cilantro and Lemon wedges
- **Nutrition Facts:** Per Serving:227cal, total fat 7.9g, carb 37.3g, Fiber 7g, Protein 6g

155.Romantic Greek Lemon Chicken Soup

Servings:2
Cooking Time: 3 Hours
Ingredients:
- ½lb of skinless Chicken Breasts
- 1 small chopped Yellow Onion
- 1 small chopped stick of Celery leaves included
- 1 clove of minced Garlic
- 1 cup of Low Sodium, Chicken Stock or Broth
- 1 cups of Water
- 2 tbsp of fresh Lemon Juice
- 1 Egg
- Sea Salt and Cracked Black Pepper to taste

Directions:
1. Place the chicken, celery, onion, garlic, stock and water in your crockpot and season it with 1 tsp of salt and ¼ of a tsp of pepper
2. Cook the chicken about 3 hours on high or 4 to 5 hours on low
3. When the chicken is cooked through and tender, take it from the cooker and allow it cool slightly
4. Slice the chicken into chunks and return it to the crockpot
5. Whisk the eggs lightly in a bowl with the lemon juice before temper them by adding several drops of hot soup at a time while constantly beating the eggs. Keep beating the eggs while adding a little hot soup until you have added about a cupful, then mix the eggs into the soup in your crockpot
6. Taste and if necessary adjust the seasoning, then serve
- **Nutrition Facts:** Per Serving:167 cal, 4g Total fat, 1g Sat fat, 99mgcho, 229 Sodium, 14g carb, 1g fiber, 20g protein

156.Homely Italian Butternut Soup With Chicken And Salami

Servings: 2
Cooking Time: 8 Hours
Ingredients:
- 1 cup of peeled and cubed Butternut Squash
- 1/2 a cup of Chicken, chopped into 1in pieces
- 1 sticks of diced Celery
- 1 small diced Carrot
- 1 small diced Onion
- 1 clove of finely chopped Garlic
- 2 tsp of Olive Oil
- 1 cup of Chicken Stock
- 1 cup of diced Tomatoes
- A pinch of grated Nutmeg
- ¼ of a tsp of Italian Seasoning
- A pinch of Red Pepper Flakes
- ¼ of a cup of diced Salami
- ¼ of a cup of Milk
- 1 Green Onion, sliced for garnishing

Directions:
1. Sauté the chicken using the oil in a pan or use the sauté option on your crockpot, until browned
2. Take out the chicken and let it cool if sautéed in the crock pot then add the squash, carrots, onions, and celery and sauté these for 3-4 minutes
3. Add the garlic and sauté until fragrant
4. Chop the chicken into cubes or strips and place everything except the salami and milk in your crockpot
5. Cook on high for 4 hours or low for 7 hours
6. Then add the milk and salami, then cook it for a further hour
7. Serve in individual soup bowls with sliced green onions as a garnish.
- **Nutrition Facts:** Per Serving:121 cal, 6.2g total fat, 11mg chol, 402mg sodium, 11.7g carb, 2.4g fiber, 5.5g protein

157.Flemish Beef Stew

Servings:8
Cooking Time: 5hours 5 Minutes
Ingredients:
- 2 lb beef, bottom round, and fat trimmed off
- ¾ lb. cremini mushroom, sliced
- 2 cups brown ale
- 1 ½ tbsp Dijon mustard
- 1 tbsp caraway seeds
- 4 tbsp canola oil
- 3 tbsp all-purpose flour
- 4 carrots, peeled and cut into inch pieces
- 1 garlic clove, minced
- 1 onion, chopped
- 1 bay leaf
- ¾ tbsp salt
- ½ tbsp ground pepper, fresh

Directions:
1. Heat two tablespoons of canola oil in a nonstick skillet. Add half of the beef and cook until brown on all sides.
2. Transfer the beef to your crockpot. Repeat the process with the remaining oil and beef.
3. Add mushrooms to the skillet and stir cook until liquid comes out and evaporates.
4. Sprinkle flour and cook without disturbing for ten seconds. Stir cook for thirty more seconds.
5. Add the brown ale and bring to boil. Cook until thick and bubbling. Transfer the mixture to the crockpot.
6. Add carrots, garlic, onions, Dijon mustard, seeds, bay leaf, salt, and pepper to the crockpot.
7. Lid the crockpot and set time for eight hours. When time is done remove the bay leaf from crockpot and serve. Enjoy.
- **Nutrition Facts:** Per Serving:Calories 301, total fats 10g saturated fats 3g, total carbs 17g, net carbs 14g, protein 31g, sugar 5g, sodium 361mg, potassium 647mg.

158.Fantastic Chicken Orzo Soup

Servings: 2
Cooking Time: 4.5 Hours
Ingredients:
- ¼lb of Chicken breasts, trimmed
- 2 cups of low-sodium Chicken Stock or Broth
- 1 Ripe chopped Tomatoes
- 1 Onion, halved and sliced
- The juice and Zest of 1 Lemon
- 1 tsp of Herbes de Provence or mixed Italian Herbs
- ½ a tsp of Sea Salt
- ½ a tsp of freshly cracked Black Pepper
- ¾ of a cup of Whole-Wheat Orzo
- ⅓ of a cup of Black or Green Olives stoned and quartered
- 1 tbsp of chopped fresh Parsley for garnish

Directions:
1. Slice the chicken into 1nch cubes
2. Place the chicken, tomatoes, onion, stock, lemon juice and zest, herbs de Provence, sea salt and black pepper in your crockpot
3. Cook covered on high for 2 hours or low for 4 hours
4. Then stir in the olives and orzo and allow it to cook a further 30 minutes
5. Allow the soup cool slightly and serve it garnished with the parsley
- **Nutrition Facts:** Per Serving:278 cal, 5g fat, 1g sat fat. 7g fiber, 29g carb, 29g protein, 63 mg chol, 434 sodium, 29g protein

159.Comforting, Traditional, Split Pea Soup

Servings: 2
Cooking Time: 8 Hours
Ingredients:
- 1 (8-ounce) pack of Dried Split Peas
- 1 large chopped Carrot
- 1 large chopped Onion
- ½ a cup of chopped Celery
- ½ a cup of Low-Sodium Diced and Cooked Ham
- 2 cups Low Sodium Chicken Broth or Stock
- 1 & 1/2 cups of Fresh Water
- Sea Salt and Black Pepper to taste
- 1 Bay Leaf

Directions:
1. Place all the ingredients in your slow cooker
2. Cook covered on the low setting for 8 hours or until the peas are tender and the soup has thickened
3. Serve
- **Nutrition Facts:** Per Serving:Cal 457, total fat 3.3g, sat fat 1.2g, Chol 25mg, sodium 309mg, carb 71.2g Fiber 27.9g, protein 36.4g

160.Split Pea Soup

Servings:10
Cooking Time: 2 Hours
Ingredients:
- 16 oz dried split peas
- 1 stalk celery, diced
- 2 large carrots, peeled and diced
- 2 cans low-fat chicken broth
- Salt and pepper to taste

Directions:
1. Rinse the peas and pick them through.
2. Place the peas in a crockpot together with celery, carrots chicken broth and water to boil.
3. Then reduce heat, simmer until peas have fallen apart, about 1 to 2 hours
4. Add salt and pepper to taste before serving.
- **Nutrition Facts:** Per Serving:Calories 65, total fats 0.3g, saturated fats 0.0g, total carbs 11.2g, net carbs 6.6g, protein 4.8g, sugar 2g, fiber 4.6g, sodium 144mg, potassium 274mg.

161.Beefed-up Vegetable Stew

Servings:6
Cooking Time: 5hours 5 Minutes
Ingredients:
- 1lb lean ground beef
- 16-ounce stew vegetables, frozen
- 14 ounce can diced tomato with garlic, basil, and oregano
- 1 cube beef broth, reduced-sodium
- ½ tbsp garlic powder
- 1 cup of water
- ½ tbsp onion powder
- ¼ tbsp black pepper

Directions:
1. Spray a nonstick skillet with cooking spray over medium heat. Brown the beef and drain it.
2. Spray your crockpot with cooking spray then add beef, stew vegetables, tomatoes, water, beef broth, garlic powder, onion powder, and black pepper.
3. Stir until well combined and cover.
4. Cook on low for five hours.
5. When the time elapses, serve and enjoy.
- **Nutrition Facts:** Per Serving:Calories 199, total fats 8.0g saturated fats 3.1g, total carbs 14g, net carbs 9.8g, protein 18g, sugar 2.2g, sodium 115mg, potassium 760mg.

162.Pork And Green Chile Stew

Servings:6
Cooking Time: 4 Hours 25 Minutes
Ingredients:
- 2 pounds boneless sirloin pork roast or shoulder roast
- 15 ounces can hominy or whole -kernel corn drained
- 2tbsp quick-cooking tapioca
- 8 ounce diced green chile peppers
- ¼ tbsp dried oregano, crushed
- 1tbsp vegetable oil
- ½ cup chopped onion, medium size
- 4cups peeled and cubed tomatoes, medium size
- 3 cups water
- 1 tbsp garlic salt
- ½ tbsp ancho chile powder
- ½ tbsp ground cumin and pepper
- ¼ tbsp dried oregano, crushed
- Chopped fresh cilantro, optional

Directions:
1. Remove excess fat from meat and cut into ½ -inch pieces
2. Add oil in large skillet and heat over medium-high heat. Sauté the onions and add half of the meat Cook until browned.
3. Remove the meat from the skillet using a slotted spoon. Repeat the process with the remaining meat.
4. Drain off fat and transfer meat to crockpot.
5. While stirring add in tomatoes, water hominy, tapioca, green chile peppers, garlic salt, ancho chili powder, cumin, ground pepper, and oregano.
6. Cover and cook on high for 4 to 5 hours or low for 7 to 8 hours.
7. Embellish each serving with cilantro.
- **Nutrition Facts:** Per Serving:Calories 180g, total fats 4g, saturated fats 1g, total carbs 23g, net carbs 20g, protein 15g, sugar 2g, fiber; 3g, sodium 251mg, potassium 782mg.

163.Delightful Thick Beef And Vegetable Soup

Servings:2
Cooking Time: 8 Hours
Ingredients:
- 1/2lb of diced Beef
- ½ a cup of Fire Roasted Diced Tomatoes
- 1 cup of Beef Stock or Broth
- 1 sliced Carrots
- 1 sliced Celery Stalks
- 1 small diced Onion
- 2 cloves of minced Garlic
- 2 tsp of crushed dried Rosemary
- 1 small bunch of baby Spinach
- Sea Salt to taste and freshly cracked Black Pepper to taste
- 1 tsp of Balsamic Vinegar

Directions:
1. Turn your Sauté option on your crockpot
2. Add the oil and when hot, add the beef
3. Sauté the beef, browning on all sides
4. Add all the other ingredients except the baby spinach and vinegar and stir to mix
5. Cook the soup covered until the beef is tender, on low for 7 to 8 hours
6. Just before serving, stir in the vinegar and baby spinach
7. Allow the soup to stand for 10 minutes, so the spinach warms through and serve
- **Nutrition Facts:** Per Serving:547 cal, 34.6g total fat, 140mg chol, 679mg sodium, 12.8g carb, 4.3g fiber, 43.7g protein

164.Delectable Chicken, Chorizo And Kale Soup

Servings:2
Cooking Time: 8 Hours
Ingredients:

- 2oz pork Chorizo without the casing (a fermented, cured, smoked sausage)
- 1 cloves of sliced Garlic
- 1 sliced Onion
- 2 cups of Chicken Stock
- 1 Bay Leaf
- 1 tsp of Sweet Paprika
- 1 medium diced Potatoes
- 2oz of thinly sliced Baby Kale
- Sea Salt and Freshly cracked Black Pepper to taste

Directions:

1. Preheat your crockpot on the sauté setting, then add the oil and sauté the onions until golden
2. Add the chorizo and the garlic, stir for about a minute and add the stock, bay leaf and potatoes
3. Cook covered for 4 to 5 hours on high or 7 to 8 hours on low
4. About 30 minutes before serving, adjust the seasoning if necessary, add the kale, give a stir and cook again for about 10 minutes
5. Then remove half of the chorizo and the bay leaf
6. Using your immersion (stick blender) or bench top blender, puree the soup, leaving just a few chunks
7. Place the remaining chorizo to the soup and serve
- **Nutrition Facts:** Per Serving:223 cal, 9.1g total fat, 2.8g sat fat, 997mg sodium, 24mg chol, 26.9 carb, 4.9g fiber, 9.9g protein

165.Easter Ham Bone Soup

Servings:10
Cooking Time: 1 Hour 55 Minutes
Ingredients:

- 1 ham bone
- 5 potatoes
- 4 cups chopped cabbage
- 2 large stalks celery, chopped
- 1 cup light whipping cream
- 12 cups water
- ⅓ Cup of all-purpose flour

Directions:

1. Put 12 cups of water and a ham bone in a crockpot and let boil until the meat comes off easily. Remove ham bone from the broth and let it cool to touch; remove meat from the bone and put in a resealable bag. Refrigerate.
2. Add broth into a mixing bowl, and refrigerate overnight. Skim any fat on top of the chilled broth and discard before transferring the broth to a large pot.
3. Bring it to boil, then add potatoes, celery, cabbage, and reserved ham, cook gently until potatoes are tender. This should take about 45 minutes.
4. Mix flour and half cup of water in a mixing bowl; blend into the potato-ham soup until consistent, add light cream and stir.
5. Serve and enjoy.
- **Nutrition Facts:** Per Serving:Calories 111, Total fats 0.2g, Saturated fat 0.0g, Total carbs 24.8g, Net carbs 21.1, Protein 3.3g, Sugar 2g, Fiber 3.7g, Sodium 33mg, Potassium 570mg.

DESSERTS AND SNACKS

166.Crockpot Sugar-free Chocolate Molten Lava Cake

Servings:12
Cooking Time: 3 Hours
Ingredients:
- 1 ½ Cup swerve sweetener, divided
- ½ cup flour, gluten-free
- 5 tbsp cocoa powder, unsweetened and divided
- 4 oz chocolate chips, sugar-free
- ½ tbsp salt
- 1 tbsp baking powder
- ½ cup butter, melted and cooled
- 3 eggs
- 3 egg yolks
- ½ tbsp vanilla liquid stevia
- 1 tbsp vanilla extract
- 2 cups hot water

Directions:
1. Grease your crockpot with cooking spray.
2. Whisk together one and a half cup swerve sweetener, flour, three tablespoon cocoa, baking powder, and salt.
3. In another mixing bowl, mix butter, eggs, egg yolks, liquid stevia, and vanilla extract.
4. Add the wet mixture to the dry mixture and mix until well combined.
5. Pour the mixture to the crockpot and top with chocolate chips.
6. Whisk together the remaining swerve sweetener and cocoa powder. Pour over the chocolate chips in the crockpot.
7. Lid the crockpot and set time for three hours. When time is done, let sit to cool.
8. Serve and enjoy.
- **Nutrition Facts:** Per Serving:Calories 157, Total Fat 13g, Saturated Fat 6.4g, Total Carbs 10.5g, Net Carbs 7.9g, Protein 3.9g, Sugar 0.2g, Fiber 2.6g, Sodium 166mg, Potassium 106mg

167.Pumpkin Muffins

Servings:5
Cooking Time: 45 Minutes
Ingredients:
- ½ cup pumpkin pieces
- 1 banana (ripe)
- 1 cup milk
- ½ tbsp pumpkin pie spice
- 2 tbsp raisins
- Cooking spray
- 1 tbsp brown sugar, granulated
- ¼ tbsp salt
- 1 egg yolk

Directions:
1. Add water and pumpkin pieces in your crockpot. Cook in high for one hour.
2. When time elapses, remove the pumpkin from the crockpot and let it rest.
3. Preheat your oven to 300ºF and spray five standard muffin cups with cooking spray.
4. Add all the ingredients in a food processor except the raisins. Blend until very smooth.
5. Stir in the raisins, then scoop the mixture into the muffin cups, then bake for forty-five minutes.
6. Let the cake rest then unmold from them from the muffin cups.
7. Serve and enjoy.
- **Nutrition Facts:** Per Serving:Calories 75, Total Fat 2g, Saturated Fat 0.5g, Total Carbs 15g, Net Carbs 14g, Protein 2g, Sugar 3g, Fiber 1g, Sodium 133mg, Potassium 70 mg

168.Chocolate Coconut Cake

Servings: 12
Cooking Time: 5 Hours
Ingredients:
- 1 ¾ cup oats
- 3 tbsp. coconut oil, melted
- ½ cup applesauce, unsweetened
- ½ cup cocoa powder, unsweetened
- ½ cup stevia
- 1 tbsp. vanilla
- ½ cup plain Greek yogurt
- ½ tsp cream of tartar
- 1 ½ tsp baking powder
- 1 ½ tsp baking soda
- ½ tsp salt
- 1 cup hot water
- ½ cup chocolate chips, sugar-free
- ¼ cup coconut flakes, unsweetened

Directions:
1. Line the crock pot with parchment paper.
2. Place all of the ingredients, except the chocolate chips and coconut, in a food processor or blender. Pulse until well combined and the oats are completely ground.
3. stir in the chocolate chips and pour evenly into the crock pot. sprinkle the coconut over the top.
4. Add the lid and cook on low heat 4-5 hours, or on high 2-3 hours, until the cake passes the toothpick test.
5. Let cool at least 15 minutes, then using the parchment paper, lift the cake from the pot and place on a wire rack to cool completely.
- **Nutrition Facts:** Per Serving: Calories 199, total Carbs 26g, net Carbs 21g, Fiber 5g, Protein 6g, Fat 10g, saturated Fat 6g, sugar 5g, sodium 224mg, Cholesterol 1mg

169.Black Bean Dip

Servings: 14
Cooking Time: 8 Hours
Ingredients:
- 2 cups dried black beans, soaked overnight
- 2 tbsp. cooking liquid
- Juice from half a lime
- ¼ tsp garlic powder
- ¼ tsp cumin
- ¼ tsp salt

Directions:
1. drain and rinse the beans and add them to the crock pot. Add just enough water to cover the beans.
2. Add the lid and cook on high 8 hours or until beans are tender.
3. drain the beans reserving 2 tablespoons of the cooking liquid.
4. Add the beans, liquid, lime juice, seasonings to a food processor and pulse until smooth.
- **Nutrition Facts:** Per Serving: Calories 122, total Carbs 22g, net Carbs 17g, Fiber 5g, Protein 8g, Fat 1g, saturated Fat 0g, sugar 1g, sodium 52mg, Cholesterol 0mg

170.Meatloaf On A Sling

Servings:4
Cooking Time: 5 Hours
Ingredients:
- ⅓ Cup ketchup
- 2 tbsp Worcestershire sauce
- 1 lb. beef, ground
- ⅔ Cup oats, quick-cooking
- 2 tbsp flaxseed, ground
- Nonstick cooking spray
- 1 tbsp water
- ½ cup onion, chopped
- ¾ cup green bell pepper, diced
- ½ cup egg substitute
- ⅛ tbsp salt

Directions:
1. Spray the crockpot with cooking spray.
2. Add ketchup Worcestershire sauce and water in a mixing bowl and mix.
3. In a separate bowl, combine beef, oats, flaxseed, onions, bell pepper, egg substitute salt, and three tablespoons of the ketchup mixture. Store the remaining ketchup in a fridge.
4. Lengthwise, fold paper foil sheets into half. Coat the strips with cooking spray then crisscross them in spoke like way. They will act as a sling.
5. Now place the meatloaf mixture at the center of the spokes.
6. Transfer the leaf to the crockpot, ensuring the aluminum foil in place for easy removal.
7. Cover the crockpot and cook on low for five hours.
8. Evenly apply the remaining ketchup mixture on the meatloaf and let it rest for fifteen minutes.
9. Carefully lift the foil strips to remove the meatloaf from the crockpot.
10. Serve and enjoy.
- **Nutrition Facts:** Per Serving:Calories 259, Total Fat 7.7g, Saturated Fat 2.8g, Total Carbs 19g, Net Carbs 15g, Protein 32g, Sugar 6.5g, Fiber 3g, Sodium 409mg, Potassium 142 mg

171.Teriyaki Meatballs

Servings: 10
Cooking Time: 4 Hours
Ingredients:
- nonstick cooking spray
- 1 lb. lean ground pork
- 1/3 cup scallion, diced fine
- 1 cup light whole wheat bread crumbs
- 1/3 cup teriyaki marinade, reduced fat, divided
- ½ tsp black pepper

Directions:
1. Heat oven to broil and spray a baking sheet with cooking spray.
2. In a large bowl, combine pork, scallion, bread crumbs, 2 tablespoons marinade, and pepper. Form into 1-inch balls and place on the prepared baking sheet. Bake 5 minutes until brown on the outside.
3. transfer the meatballs to the crock pot and pour the remaining marinade over the top. stir gently to coat.
4. Add the lid and cook on low heat 4 hours, stirring occasionally. serve warm.
- **Nutrition Facts:** Per Serving: Calories 152, total Carbs 7g, net Carbs 6g, Fiber 1g, Protein 10g, Fat 10g, saturated Fat 4g, sugar 2g, sodium 239mg, Cholesterol 33mg

172.Scrumptious Buffalo Chicken Meatballs

Servings: 2
Cooking Time:2 Hours
Ingredients:
- ¼lb of ground Chicken
- ¼ of a cup of Panko (Breadcrumbs)
- 1 Egg
- 1/8 of a tsp of Garlic Powder
- 1/8 of a tsp of Onion Powder
- 1 thinly sliced Green Onion
- Sea Salt to taste
- Ground Black Pepper to taste
- ¼ of a cup of Buffalo Sauce
- ¼ of a cup of Blue Dressing

Directions:
1. Place all the ingredients except the buffalo and blue cheese sauce in a bowl and mix them together
2. Make the mixture into 12 equal sized balls and place them in your crockpot
3. Cover them in buffalo sauce and cook, covered, for 2 hours on high
4. Serve with the blue cheese
- **Nutrition Facts:** Per Serving:Cal 273, Total fat 11.3g, sat fat 2.5g, cho95.6mg, Sodium 976.3mg, Carb 23g, Protein 15.5g

173.Raspberry Oat Snack Bars

Servings: 16
Cooking Time: 4 Hours
Ingredients:
- nonstick cooking spray
- 1 cup white whole wheat flour
- 1 cup oats
- ½ cup stevia
- ½ tsp baking powder
- ¼ tsp salt
- ½ cup coconut oil, melted
- 2/3 cup raspberry jam, sugar-free

Directions:
1. spray the crock pot with cooking spray.
2. In a large bowl, whisk together flour, oats, stevia, baking powder, and salt.
3. stir in the coconut oil. Press half the mixture on the bottom of the crock pot.
4. Carefully spread the jam over the bottom crust and sprinkle remaining oat mixture evenly over the top, press lightly.
5. Add the lid and cook on low heat 4 hours or until the bars are set and starting to brown around the edges.
6. Let cool 15 minutes before slicing and transferring to a wire rack to cool completely.
- **Nutrition Facts:** Per Serving: Calories 212, total Carbs 20g, net Carbs 18g, Fiber 2g, Protein 2g, Fat 14g, saturated Fat 12g, sugar 6g, sodium 59mg, Cholesterol 0mg

174.Forbidden Chocolate Lava Cake

Servings: 2
Cooking Time: 3 Hours

Ingredients:

- 1/4 cup of Flour
- 1/2 tsp of Baking Powder
- 2 tbsp of Dutch Bakers Chocolate
- 2 tbsp of Unsalted Butter
- 1oz of Semisweet Dutch Chocolate
- 1/3 of a cup of Powered Erythritol
- 2 tbsp of Dutch Cocoa Powder
- 1 tsp of Pure Vanilla Extract
- 1/8 tsp of Sea Salt
- 1/4 of a cup of Milk
- 1 Egg Yolk
- 1/4 cup Dutch-processed cocoa powder
- 1/4 Powered Erythritol
- 1/8 of a cup Brown Sugar
- 3/4 of a cup of hot water, add more if needed

Directions:

1. Place a liner inside your crockpot or spray the inside with non-stick spray
2. Mix together the flour and baking powder in a bowl
3. Melt together the butter and chocolate together on low power in a microwave
4. Whisk 1/3 of a cup of powered erythritol, 2 tbsp of cocoa powder, the milk, egg yolk, vanilla into the chocolate butter mixture
5. Then add the flour mixture
6. Pour the batter into your lined crockpot and smooth the surface
7. Whisk together the cocoa powder, powered erythritol, brown sugar and hot water until completely combined. Carefully pour the mixture onto the center of the batter in your slow cooker, but do not mix them
8. Cover your crockpot with 3 layers of paper towels and
9. Cook, covered, for 2-3 hours on HIGH, check the progress after 2 hours. When done the cake will come away from the sides of your crockpot bowl
10. Remove the lid carefully and allow it to cool for 30 minutes
11. Serve the cake topped with ice cream or whipped cream
- **Nutrition Facts:** Per Serving:Cal 335, total fat 17.7g, sat fat 10.7g, chol 140mg, sodium 223mg, carb 39g, fiber 0.08g, protein 4.9gg

175.Deviled Eggs

Servings:12
Cooking Time: 1 Hour 30 Minutes
Ingredients:
- 6 eggs
- 2 tbsp light mayonnaise
- ⅛ tbsp mustard powder
- 1 black pepper, freshly ground
- 1 pinch salt
- I scallion, sliced (for garnish)
- Grape tomatoes (for garnish)

Directions:
1. Place the eggs in your crockpot and add water such that the eggs are covered.
2. Set the timer for two and a half hours on HIGH.
3. When time is over, remove from crockpot and place the eggs in ice-cold water. Peel the eggs cut them vertically.
4. Remove the yolks and place them in a mixing bowl. Add mayonnaise, mustard powder pepper, and salt, then mash using a folk.
5. Fill the egg whites with the mayo mixture and garnish with scallions and grape tomatoes.
6. Serve and enjoy.
- **Nutrition Facts:** Per Serving:Calories 45, Total Fat 3g, Saturated Fat 1g, Total Carbs 1g, Net Carbs 0g, Protein 3g, Sugar 0g, Fiber 0g, Sodium 70mg, Potassium 35 mg

176.Dreamy Cinnamon Cheesecake

Servings: 2
Cooking Time: 4 Hours
Ingredients:
- 1/3 of a cup of Graham Cracker crumbs
- 1 tbsp of melted Unsalted Butter
- 1/8 of a tsp of Cinnamon
- Sea Salt as needed
- 6oz of Cream Cheese, at room temperature
- ½ a tbsp of All-purpose Flour
- 1 large Egg
- 1 tsp of Pure Almond Extract
- ½ a cup of Sour Cream

Directions:
1. Mix together the cracker crumbs, a pinch of salt, cinnamon and melted butter
2. Use a spring-form baking dish that will fit inside your crockpot on a stand
3. Spread the base mixture over the bottom and up the sides of the baking dish
4. Beat the flour ¼ of a tsp of salt and cream cheese together, then add the extract, egg and sour cream, beat these until smooth
5. Pour the cheesecake into the baking dish
6. Place half an inch of water in your crockpot and insert the stand
7. Place the cheesecake in the center without the sides touching the bowl
8. Place a triple layer of paper kitchen towels over the crockpot and close the lid
9. Cook on high for 2 hours without opening
10. Turn off the heat and keeping the lid closed (so you do not lose any heat), allow the cheesecake to cool for about an hour before taking it out and cooling further to room temperature
11. Place the cheesecake wrapped in plastic, in the refrigerator (it will absorb smells if not wrapped) for about 4 hours
12. Carefully remove the cheesecake from the baking dish, then serve with your favorite toppings
- **Nutrition Facts:** Per Serving:Cal 362, total fat 34.5g, sat fat 21g, chol 154mg, carb 6.5g, fiber 0.2g, protein 7.9

177.No Peel Crockpot Hard-boiled Eggs

Servings:8
Cooking Time: 1 Hour 30 Minutes
Ingredients:
- 8 eggs
- Unsalted butter

Directions:
1. Add two cups of water in your crockpot.
2. Butter an oven-safe bowl that fits your crockpot. Break the eggs to the buttered bowl ensuring the yolks don't break.
3. Cover and cook for an hour and a half or until the eggs look hard-boiled.
4. Loosen the edges with a spatula then remove the safe bowl from the crockpot.
5. Turn the bowl on a cutting board and chop the eggs to your desired consistency.
6. Serve and enjoy the eggs with a salad of choice.
- **Nutrition Facts:** Per Serving:Calories 63, Total Fat 4g, Saturated Fat 1g, Total Carbs 1g, Net Carbs 0g, Protein 6g, Sugar 1g, Fiber 0.1g, Sodium 62 mg, Potassium 61 mg

178.Skinny Pecan Pie

Servings: 16
Cooking Time: 4 Hours
Ingredients:
- nonstick cooking spray
- 1 (9-inch) whole wheat pie crust
- 1/2 cup honey for a mildly sweet pie OR 3/4 cup honey for a moderately sweet pie
- 3 egg whites, whipped with a fork
- 2 cups diced pecans
- 4 teaspoons vanilla extract
- 1 teaspoon cinnamon
- 3 tablespoons cornstarch or white whole wheat flour

Directions:
1. spray the crock pot with cooking spray. Line the bottom with a piece of parchment paper.
2. Place the pie crust in the crock pot and mold it to fit the inside.
3. In a large bowl, beat together all the ingredients until well combined.
4. Pour the filling into the crust. Use a knife to carefully cut away the excess crust at the top.
5. Place two sheets of paper towels over the top of the crock pot and add the lid. Cook on low heat 3 hours.
6. Remove the lid and the paper towels and continue cooking, without the lid, for another 60 minutes.
7. Carefully use a knife to loosen the pie around the edges. Once the pie is loose, carefully remove the pie and transfer to a serving plate to cool completely.
- **Nutrition Facts:** Per Serving: Calories 205, total Carbs 20g, net Carbs 17g, Fiber 3g, Protein 4g, Fat 14g, saturated Fat 1g, sugar 9g, sodium 85mg, Cholesterol 0mg

179.Seafood Supreme Dip

Servings: 2
Cooking Time: 2 Hours
Ingredients:

- ¼ of a cup of cream of Shrimp Soup
- ¼ of a cup of grated Tasty Cheddar Cheese
- ¼ of a cup of grated American Cheese
- ¼ of a cup of cooked diced Lobster
- ¼ of a cup of chopped cooked Shrimp or Crab Meat
- A dash of Paprika
- A dash of Nutmeg
- A dash of Cayenne Pepper
- A loaf of French or Crusty Bread, cubed for dipping

Directions:

1. Place everything except the cubed bread in your crockpot and cook, covered, on high for 2 hours, stirring occasionally
- **Nutrition Facts:** Per Serving:Cal 115, total fat 3.5g, sat fat 1.4g, unsat 1g, chol 34mg, carb 12.7, sodium 427mg, protein 7.7g

180.Devils Drumsticks

Servings: 2
Cooking Time: 3 To 6 Hours
Ingredients:

- Chicken Drumsticks
- ¼ of a cup of Chili Salsa
- 2 tsp of Hot Chili Sauce (more if you like it really hot)
- 1 tsp of Smoked Paprika
- ¼ of a tsp of Dried Thyme
- 1 Bay Leaf
- 2 tsp of Olive Oil

Directions:

1. Place all the ingredients in your crockpot and mix them well
2. Cook, covered, on low for 6 hours or high for 3 hours
3. Serve with the sauce in the crockpot
- **Nutrition Facts:** Per Serving:Cal 209, total fat 9g. sat fat 2g chol98mg, sodium536mg, carb 3g, protein 27g

181.Chocolate Quinoa Brownies

Servings:2
Cooking Time: 4 Hours
Ingredients:
- 1 cup of cooked Quinoa
- 1 small Egg
- ½ a tsp of Vanilla Extract
- ¾ of a cup of Sugar Free Chocolate Chips
- 2 tbsp of Unsweetened Cocoa Powder
- A large pinch of Sea Salt
- 1/8 of a tsp of Baking Powder
- 1/8 of a cup of ground Flaxseed
- ¼ of a cup of Unsweetened Apple Sauce
- 1/4 of a cup of Heavy Cream
- 1/4 of a cup of Unsweetened Cocoa Powder
- 1 tsp of Liquid Chocolate Stevia
- ½ a tsp of Vanilla Extract

Directions:
1. Process all the ingredients together in your food processor and allow it to rest while you line your crockpot bottom with parchment paper
2. Pour and spread the mixture on the parchment paper and smooth over the surface
3. Cook, covered, for 2 hours on high or 4 hours on low
4. Cool on a wire rack, then frost and slice into portions
5. Frosting
6. Combine all the ingredients and melt over a lot heat or in your microwave
- **Nutrition Facts:** Per Serving:Cal 149, total fat 4.2g, sat fat 0.8g, sodium 19mg, Carb 22.1g
- Fiber 2.9g, protein 5.6g

182.Eggplant & Spinach Dip

Servings: 8
Cooking Time: 3 Hours
Ingredients:
- 1 eggplant, peeled and cubed
- 1 tbsp. olive oil, divided
- ¼ tsp salt
- 2 cups baby spinach
- 3 cloves garlic, diced fine
- 1/3 cup fat-free parmesan cheese, grated
- nonstick cooking spray

Directions:
1. Heat oven to 400°F. Line a baking sheet with foil.
2. In a large bowl, add the eggplant, ½ tablespoon oil, and salt and toss to coat. spread in an even layer on the baking sheet and cook 10-15 minutes or until the eggplant starts to brown.
3. Heat the remaining oil in a large skillet over medium heat. Add the spinach and garlic and cook until spinach is wilted about 3 minutes.
4. Place the roasted eggplant in a food processor and pulse until smooth. If the mixture is too thick, add a tablespoon of water, one at a time, until the mixture is smooth and creamy.
5. Add the spinach and half the parmesan to the eggplant and pulse just until combined.
6. spray the crock pot with cooking spray.
7. transfer the eggplant mixture to the crock pot, add the lid, and cook on how to heat 3 hours, or until hot and bubbly.
8. sprinkle the remaining parmesan over the top and serve.
- **Nutrition Facts:** Per Serving: Calories 58, total Carbs 6g, net Carbs3 g, Fiber 3g, Protein 3g, Fat 3g, saturated Fat 1g, sugar 3g, sodium 131mg, Cholesterol 3mg

183.Cinnamon Mixed Nuts

Servings: 12
Cooking Time: 1 ½ Hours
Ingredients:
- 1 cup almonds
- 1 cup pecans
- 1 cup walnuts
- 1 ½ tsp cinnamon
- 1/3 cup honey

Directions:
1. Place the nuts in the crock pot.
2. sprinkle cinnamon over the top and add honey. stir well to make sure all the nuts are coated.
3. Add the lid and cook on low heat 1-1/2 hours. serve warm.
- **Nutrition Facts:** Per Serving: Calories 171, total Carbs 12g, net Carbs 9g, Fiber 3g, Protein 4g, Fat 13g, saturated Fat 1g, sugar 9g, sodium 1mg, Cholesterol 0mg

184.Key Lime Dump Cake

Servings:4
Cooking Time: 2 Hours
Ingredients:
- 44 oz Key lime filling
- 15 ¼ oz Betty Crocker Vanilla Cake mix
- Cooking spray
- 8 tbsp butter, melted

Directions:
1. Spray the crockpot with cooking spray then spread the lime filling at the bottom.
2. Combine the cake mix and butter in a mixing bowl.
3. Pour the mixture over lime filling and spread it evenly.
4. Cover the crockpot with the lid and set time for two hours.
5. When time elapses, serve and enjoy with whip cream.
- **Nutrition Facts:** Per Serving:Calories 197, Total Fat 23g, Saturated Fat 4g, Total Carbs 18g, Net Carbs 16g, Protein 3.4g, Sugar 23g, Fiber 0.3g, Sodium 296mg, Potassium 63mg

185.Flavorful Cranberry Cheesecake

Servings: 2
Cooking Time: 4 Hours
Ingredients:
- 4oz of Cream Cheese, softened
- 1 Eggs
- ½ a cup of Greek Yogurt
- 1/3 of a cup of Graham Cracker Crumbed
- 1 tbsp of Raw Sugar
- ½ a tsp of Pure Vanilla Extract
- ½ a tbsp of Flour
- 1 tbsp of melted Unsalted Butter
- ¼ of a tsp of Sea Salt
- 1 1/2 cups of fresh Cranberries (or other Berries if preferred)
- The juice and zest of one Lemon
- 1 tbsp of Cornstarch
- 1 very ripe Banana (for sweetening unless the berries are sweet)
- 1/4 a cup of Pure Water

Directions:
1. Beat together the flour, salt, vanilla and cream cheese until there are no lumps
2. Add the eggs and yogurt, beating continuously until they are completely incorporated
3. Mix the crumbed crackers and butter together and mold this into the spring form dish that fits inside your crockpot
4. Pour the cream cheese mixture onto the crust in the spring form dish
5. Place half an inch of water in the crockpot and the stand
6. Place the cheesecake on the stand and cover it with 3 sheets of kitchen towels
7. Cook, covered, for 2 hours and do not open. Turn off and let cool unopened for an hour
8. Place the cheesecake on wire rack to cool the in the refrigerator for 4 hours
9. Beat together the topping and spread it on the cooled cheesecake before serving
- **Nutrition Facts:** Per Serving:Cal 651, total fat 34.9g, sat fat 2.1g, chol 154mg, sodium 367mg, carb 67.1g. fiber 3g, protein 17.2g

186. Glazed Tropical Cookie Bars

Servings: 25
Cooking Time: 4 Hours
Ingredients:
- nonstick cooking spray
- 1 ½ + 1/3 cup flour
- ¾ cup splenda, divided
- 1/8 tsp salt
- ¾ cup butter, cubed
- 2 eggs
- ½ cup low-fat sour cream
- 20 oz. can crushed pineapple, drained well
- ½ cup stevia confectioners' sugar
- 1 tbsp. skim milk
- ½ tsp coconut extract

Directions:
1. spray the crock pot with cooking spray.
2. In a large bowl, combine 1 ½ cups flour, ¼ cup splenda, salt, and butter until mixture resembles coarse crumbs. Reserve 1 cup of the mixture. Press remaining mixture in an even layer on the bottom of the crock pot.
3. In a separate large bowl, whisk together eggs, sour cream, remaining flour, and splenda until well combined.
4. stir in pineapples and spread over crust in the crock pot.
5. sprinkle the reserved crumb mixture over the top of the filling. Place two paper towels over the top and add the lid.
6. Cook on low heat 4 hours, or on high 2 hours, until filling is set and the edges start to brown.
7. Let cool before slicing and transferring to a wire rack.
8. In a small bowl, whisk together the stevia powdered sugar, milk, and coconut extract until smooth. drizzle over bars.
- **Nutrition Facts:** Per Serving: Calories 119, total Carbs 13g, net Carbs 12g, Fiber 1g, Protein 2g, Fat 7g, saturated Fat 2g, sugar 6g, sodium 72mg, Cholesterol 16mg

187. Savory Blue Cheese Dip

Servings: 2
Cooking Time: 2 Hours
Ingredients:
- 2oz of grated Gruyere Cheese
- 3oz of Blue Cheese
- ¼ of a cup of Hot Salsa Sauce
- ¼ of a cup of finely sliced Sautéed Mushrooms
- 3 cloves of minced Garlic
- ¼ of a tsp of Ground Black Pepper

Directions:
1. Place everything in your crockpot and stir to combine, then cook, covered, on high for 1 to 2 hours
- **Nutrition Facts:** Per Serving:Cal 89, total fat 4g, Chol 16mg, Sodium 601mg, Carb 5g, protein 8g

188.Pumpkin Streusel Bars

Servings: 16
Cooking Time: 4 Hours

Ingredients:

- nonstick cooking spray
- 1 1/3 cups white whole wheat flour, divided
- 1 tsp baking powder
- ½ tsp baking soda
- 1 tsp cinnamon, divided
- 1/8 tsp ginger
- ¼ tsp salt
- 1 cup stevia, divided
- 2 eggs
- ½ cup coconut oil, melted
- ½ can pumpkin puree
- ½ teaspoon vanilla
- 4 tbsp. butter, unsalted

Directions:

1. spray the crock pot with cooking spray.
2. In a medium bowl, whisk together 1 cup flour, baking powder, baking soda, ½ teaspoon cinnamon, ginger, and salt until combined.
3. In a large bowl, beat together the eggs, stevia, oil, pumpkin, and vanilla until light and frothy.
4. Add the dry ingredients and continue mixing until combined. Pour batter evenly in the crock pot.
5. In a small bowl, use a fork to mix the remaining 1/3 cup flour, ¼ cup stevia, ½ teaspoon cinnamon, and butter until combined. sprinkle evenly over the top of the batter.
6. Add the lid and cook on low heat 3-4 hours, or on high 2-3 hours or until the bars pass the toothpick test.
7. Let cool 15 minutes before slicing and serving.
- **Nutrition Facts:** Per Serving: Calories 150, total Carbs 19g, net Carbs 18g, Fiber 1g, Protein 2g, Fat 8g, saturated Fat 2g, sugar 2g, sodium 83mg, Cholesterol 22mg

189. Amazing Carrot Cake

Servings: 2
Cooking Time: 3 Hours
Ingredients:
- ¾ of a cup of Unsweetened Applesauce
- 2 very ripe Bananas
- 1 large egg, at room temperature
- 1/2 a cup of Flour
- 1 tsp of Baking Soda
- 1½ tsp of Baking Powder
- ½ a tsp of Sea Salt
- 1 tsp of Ground Cinnamon
- 2 cups of Grated Carrots
- ½ a cup of Shredded Coconut
- ½ a cup of Chopped Nuts of your choice
- ½ a tsp of Pure Vanilla Extract
- ½ a cup of unsweetened Crushed Pineapple, with juice
- 2 tbsp of Unsalted Butter (softened)
- 4oz of Cream Cheese (softened)
- 1 tsp of Pure Vanilla Extract
- ¼ of a cup of Powered Erythritol

Directions:
1. Oil a cake tin that will fit inside your crockpot
2. Whisk together the eggs, sugar and applesauce with the baking powder, baking soda, flour, cinnamon and salt
3. Stir in the carrots, nuts, coconut, pineapple and vanilla extract
4. Gently pour the batter into the cake tin and place in your crockpot
5. Place three folded paper towels over the top of the slow cooker
6. Cook, covered, on low for 3 hours the check using a toothpick inserted in the center
7. Allow the cake cool completely before frosting
8. Cream Cheese Frosting
9. Beat the cream cheese and butter together until it's fluffy
10. Add in the powered Erythritol and vanilla, then beat it until it becomes nice and smooth
11. Frost the cake when it's completely cooled, cutting into the layers if desired
12. Top with toasted coconut
- **Nutrition Facts:** Per Serving:Cal 460, total fat 16.6g, chol 8.6g, sodium 200mg, carb 75.1g, fiber 2.3g, protein 5.7g

190.Heavenly Poached Pears

Servings: 2
Cooking Time: 3 Hours
Ingredients:
- 4 small Pears, skinned but with the stem
- ½ a cup of fresh Apple Juice
- 1 Stick of Cinnamon
- 2 tbsp of chopped Walnuts

Directions:
1. Slice a small section from the base of each pear so it will stand on its end
2. Place the apple juice in your crockpot with the cinnamon stick and lay each pear on its side in the juice
3. Cook, covered, for 1 hour on low, then turn the pears over and cook, covered for another hour or until tender
4. When cooked, place the pears on plates
5. Pass the liquid through a sieve into a saucepan
6. Simmer the sauce with the cinnamon stick and walnuts until it's reduced to a nice consistency
7. Pour the sauce over the pears and serve
- **Nutrition Facts:** Per Serving:236 cal, 6.9g total fat, 0.6g sat fat, 4mg sodium, 38.3g carb, 8.5g fiber, 4.6 protein

191.Delightful Peach Cobbler

Servings: 2
Cooking Time: 4 Hours
Ingredients:
- 1.1/2 cups of peeled and sliced frozen or fresh Peaches
- 1 very ripe Banana
- 1/2 a tsp of Ground Cinnamon
- 1 cup of Grahame Crackers
- 1 tbsp of Raw Sugar
- 1/2 a tsp of Ground Cinnamon
- 1/4 of a tsp of Ground Nutmeg
- 1 tsp of pure Vanilla Extract
- 1/2 a cup of Cashew Milk

Directions:
1. Insert a liner into your crockpot or spray it with non-stick spray
2. Combine the peaches, banana and cinnamon in a bowl, then spread them in your crockpot
3. Mix together the graham crackers, vanilla, sugar, nutmeg, cinnamon, and milk, stir it thoroughly until smooth
4. Spread this mixture evenly over peaches
5. Place 3 thicknesses of paper towels to stop condensation over the cobbler
6. Cook, covered, on low setting for 3-4 hours, or until set
- **Nutrition Facts:** Per Serving:Cal 181, total fat 5.4g, sat fat, 1.5g, chol 2mg, Sodium 393mg, carb 32g, fiber 1.8g, protein 4.1g

192.Creme Brulee

Servings:4
Cooking Time: 2 Hours
Ingredients:
- 4 egg yolks
- ¼ cup white sugar
- 1 ⅔ cups whipping cream, heavy
- 2 tbsp vanilla extract
- ¼ tbsp salt

Directions:
1. In a mixing bowl, whisk together egg yolks, quarter cup sugar, and salt.
2. Whisk in whipping cream and vanilla extract. Strain the custard mixture into a measuring cup.
3. Line the crockpot bottom with folded kitchen towel. Place the ramekins on the towel and fill the crockpot with water such that the water comes halfway the ramekins.
4. Pour the custard mixture into ramekins then drape the towel over the crockpot. Place the lid the crockpot.
5. Set the timer for two hours so that the custard jiggles a little bit but is set.
6. Remove the ramekins from the crockpot and let them rest to completely cool.
- **Nutrition Facts:** Per Serving:Calories 255, Total Fat 41.1g, Saturated Fat 24g, Total Carbs 20g, Net Carbs 0g, Protein 4.7g, Sugar 4g, Fiber 0g, Sodium 191mg, Potassium 96mg

193.Turkey Breasts

Servings:4
Cooking Time: 6 Hours
Ingredients:
- 1 turkey breast
- 1 tbsp garlic powder
- 1 tbsp paprika
- 1 tbsp parsley

Directions:
1. Place the turkey breast in a crockpot.
2. Season with garlic, parsley, and paprika. Let sit to marinate for five minutes.
3. Set timer for six hours. When the time elapses, remove the turkey from the crockpot and place it on a cutting board.
4. Cover with aluminum foil and let rest for ten minutes.
5. Cut into pieces and serve. Enjoy.
- **Nutrition Facts:** Per Serving:Calories 140, Total Fat 3g, Saturated Fat 1g, Total Carbs 0g, Net Carbs 0g, Protein 27g, Sugar 0g, Fiber 0g, Sodium 41mg, Potassium 42 mg

194.Cardamom Apple Bread Pudding

Servings: 6
Cooking Time: 4 Hours
Ingredients:
- Butter flavored cooking spray
- 6 slices whole-wheat bread, cut in 1-inch cubes
- 1 ½ cups coconut milk, reduced fat
- 3 eggs, lightly beaten
- 1 cup applesauce, unsweetened
- ¾ tsp cardamom
- 1 tsp cinnamon
- ¼ tsp nutmeg
- 1 cup apples, peel, core & chop

Directions:
1. spray the crock pot with cooking spray.
2. Place the bread, in an even layer, in the pot.
3. In a large bowl, whisk together milk, eggs, applesauce, and spices until well combined.
4. Fold in the apples and pour the mixture evenly over the bread, pressing gently to make sure all of the bread is covered.
5. Add the lid and cook on low heat 4-5 hours, or on high 2-3 hours or until the pudding passes the toothpick test. Let cool at least 15 minutes before serving.
- **Nutrition Facts:** Per Serving: Calories 256, total Carbs 23g, net Carbs 20g, Fiber 3g, Protein 8g, Fat 16g, saturated Fat 12g, sugar 7g, sodium 190mg, Cholesterol 93mg

195.Butterscotch Almond Brownies

Servings: 24
Cooking Time: 3 Hours
Ingredients:
- nonstick cooking spray
- 1 cup butter, soft
- 3 cups splenda brown sugar blend
- 4 eggs
- 3 tbsp. vanilla
- 1 ½ cups flour
- 3 teaspoons baking powder
- 1 ½ cups almonds, chopped

Directions:
1. spray crock pot with cooking spray.
2. In a large bowl, beat butter and splenda until creamy.
3. Add eggs and vanilla and mix to combine.
4. stir in remaining ingredients until combined.
5. spread the batter evenly in the pot. Add the lid and cook on low 2-3 hours until brownies pass the toothpick test. Let cool completely before slicing.
- **Nutrition Facts:** Per Serving: Calories 182, total Carbs 14g, net Carbs 10g, Fiber 4g, Protein 6g, Fat 12g, saturated Fat 2g, sugar 1g, sodium 138mg, Cholesterol 0mg

196.Peanut Butter Chocolate Cake

Servings: 16
Cooking Time: 4 Hours
Ingredients:
- nonstick cooking spray
- 1 cup whole wheat pastry flour
- ½ cup cocoa powder, unsweetened
- 1 tbsp. baking powder
- ½ cup honey
- 2 egg whites
- 1/3 cup peanut butter, sugar-free
- 2 tsp vanilla
- ¾ cup apple sauce, unsweetened

Directions:
1. Line the bottom of the crock pot with parchment paper and spray with cooking spray.
2. In a large bowl, whisk together flour, cocoa powder, and baking powder until combined.
3. In a separate bowl, whisk together honey, egg whites, peanut butter, vanilla, and applesauce.
4. stir the dry ingredients into the honey mixture until well combined.
5. Pour the batter into the crock pot and add the lid. Cook on low heat 4 hours, or until the cake passes the toothpick test.
6. Let cool 15 minutes in the pot before transferring to a wire rack to cool completely.
- **Nutrition Facts:** Per Serving: Calories 141, total Carbs 19g, net Carbs 16g, Fiber 3g, Protein 3g, Fat 3g, saturated Fat 2g, sugar 10g, sodium 0mg, Cholesterol 0mg

197.Autumn Baked Apples

Servings: 6
Cooking Time: 5 Hours
Ingredients:
- 6 Granny smith apples, cored
- ½ cup cranberries, dried
- ½ cup walnuts, coarsely chopped
- 2 tbsp. stevia brown sugar
- 1 tbsp. orange zest
- 1 cup water

Directions:
1. Peel just the top ¼ of each apple.
2. In a small bowl, combine cranberries, walnuts, stevia, and orange zest and mix well.
3. stuff the mixture into the apples and place them in the crock pot.
4. Pour the water around the apples. Add the lid and cook on low heat 4-5 hours.
- **Nutrition Facts:** Per Serving: Calories 186, total Carbs 27g, net Carbs 21g, Fiber 6g, Protein 2g, Fat 7g, saturated Fat 1g, sugar 26g, sodium 5mg, Cholesterol 0mg

198.Chocolate Chip Scones

Servings:2
Cooking Time: 3 Hours
Ingredients:
- 125g of Self Raising Flour
- A pinch of salt
- 26g of Unsalted Butter, cubed
- 15g of Caster Sugar
- 75ml of Milk, any kind
- 50 g no sugar, chocolate chips
- Any additional fillings you desire such as Sultanas, Blueberries, dried Cranberries

Directions:
1. Mix together the flour, salt and sugar in a bowl
2. Rub the butter into the flour mixture
3. Stir in the milk to form a soft dough
4. Add the chocolate chips and any other fillings you desire
5. Form the dough in a round shape that will fit into your slow cooker
6. Divide the top of the dough with a knife, making 6 large or 12 small equal segments
7. Place a liner or oil the inside of your crockpot and place the dough inside
8. Put 3 sheets of kitchen towel right on top of your crockpot
9. Cook, covered, on high for approx 1 5 hours on high or 3 hours on low
10. Remove from the cooker and allow to cool, then slice into triangles
- **Nutrition Facts:** Per Serving:Cal 473, total fat 17.2g, sat fat 8.8g, Chol 31mg, sodium162mg, carb 73.8g, fiber 1.7g, protein 8.9g

199.Special Barbecue Kielbasa

Servings: 2
Cooking Time: 4 Hours
Ingredients:
- ½lb of Kielbasa, sliced into ½ inch rings
- 1 cup of Ketchup
- 1 tsp of Worcestershire Sauce
- 1 tsp of Creole Mustard
- 1 tsp of Hot Sauce (more or less to taste)
- 1 small diced Onion
- ¼ of a cup of Bourbon

Directions:
1. Combine all the ingredients and cook, covered, on low for 4 hours
- **Nutrition Facts:** Per Serving:Cal.495, Fat 25.7g, sat fat10.1g, Chol125mg, Sodium2605mg, carb 35.2g, fiber 1.6g protein 25.2g

200.Broccoli Cheese Dip

Servings: 10
Cooking Time: 3 Hours

Ingredients:

- 1 tsp extra virgin olive oil
- 1 onion, diced fine
- 6 cups broccoli florets
- 10 ½ oz. can condensed broccoli cheese soup
- 1 cup cheddar cheese, grated
- ½ cup skim milk
- ½ cup sour cream
- 1 tbsp. Worcestershire sauce
- 1 tsp garlic powder
- 1 tsp basil

Directions:

1. Heat the oil in a large skillet over med-high heat.
2. Add the onion and cook until translucent, about 5 minutes.
3. Add the broccoli and cook, occasionally stirring, another 5 minutes. Remove from heat.
4. Add the remaining ingredients to the crock pot and stir to combine. Add the broccoli and onions and stir well.
5. Add the lid and cook on low heat 2-3 hours until cheese is melted and broccoli is tender. stir well before serving.
- **Nutrition Facts:** Per Serving: Calories 124, total Carbs 8g, net Carbs 7g, Fiber 1g, Protein 6g, Fat 8g, saturated Fat 4g, sugar 2g, sodium 326mg, Cholesterol 20mg